DESIGNING A HOUSE

An inexpensive porch keeps out the rain and makes an inviting transitional entry between outside and in.

DESIGNING A HOUSE
THE ILLUSTRATED GUIDE TO PLANNING YOUR OWN HOME

LESTER WALKER

THE OVERLOOK PRESS
NEW YORK, NY

This edition first published in hardcover in the United States in 2012 by The Overlook Press,
Peter Mayer Publishers, Inc.
141 Wooster Street
New York, NY 10012
www.overlookpress.com
For bulk and special sales, please contact sales@overlookny.com

Cataloging-in-Publication Data is available from the Library of Congress

Book design by Lester Walker
Printed in China
ISBN 978-1-59020-139-8

1 3 5 7 9 10 8 6 4 2

To my wife Karen, my sons Jess and Andrew, and my niece Tenille

and

The Valeo Family: Tom, Lois, Tom Jr., Anna, and in loving memory of Phoebe

  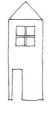   

CONTENTS

A tiny sitting area with lots of light works well in a residual space in almost any home design.

1 INTRODUCTION

This brief chapter contains a few thoughts regarding the ideas in this book and an introduction to Lois, Tom, and Anna Sample, the family who will illustrate these ideas by designing their own house for us to see.

DO ALL THESE PEOPLE HAVE THE SAME LIFESTYLE ?

BE YOUR OWN ARCHITECT

So you want to design your own home, and you're not interested in the ubiquitous "McMansion," or one of the standard builder's homes we see dotting the American landscape. Instead, you want a house that works for your particular needs, that relates to your site, and that reflects your values and personality. And you want to embrace the process of creating your dream house, seeing it as one of the most satisfying adventures you will ever experience. Learning some basic principles before you begin will ease the process of making your dreams a reality. And the final result will be the unique pleasure of living in a home you designed yourself.

Architects are professionals who have studied and trained for years before beginning to work with clients. It requires a great deal of experience to develop a set of building plans that make their clients happy. One of the most time-consuming aspects of the architect's job is devising a complete program of the client's needs. Ultimately, if done well, a design is developed that fits the owner's style of living, budget, and personal taste. The architect's fees will generally be around 10% of the cost of construction, some charging more, some less. Whichever it is, it's not a trifling amount.

The first principle of good design, which most architects start with, is "form follows function": the architect must define function before he or she begins to give form. To that end, the architect must become well acquainted with the client so that the final product is a house that is perfectly suited. *The more personal the program, the more livable the house will be. No one can outline a more personal program (and, if provided with the proper tools, no one can design a more personal home) for themselves than you.*

This book, then, is a step-by-step guide (with a little humor thrown in) for people who want to save the cost of an architect, or for those who would like to take their own plans to an architect for a final "stamp of approval." One note of caution: building codes and municipal laws have tightened considerably in recent years. You may need the help of an architect or engineer simply to comply with your local building code. This can be easily addressed by hiring, on a limited basis, a good architect or contractor familiar with your town's laws and regulations. He or she may need to enhance your drawings or complete a new set of drawings to gain a permit for construction.

We are indeed fortunate to live in the age of the internet, where you will find a wealth of information and resources to assist you in designing your home. Add to that the many magazines devoted to the home which you can peruse for ideas. There are also many books on the market that discuss what good design entails.

Everything you need is at your fingertips. Let the journey begin!

ONCE UPON A TIME THERE WAS A LONG THIN SNAKE WHO LIVED IN A LONG THIN HOUSE.

HE MARRIED A SHORT FAT SOW WHO LIVED IN A SHORT FAT HOUSE.

THE LONG THIN SNAKE COULD NOT GET COMFORTABLE IN THE SHORT FAT SOW'S SHORT FAT HOUSE.

THE SHORT FAT SOW COULD NOT FIT THROUGH THE DOORWAY OF THE LONG THIN SNAKE'S LONG THIN HOUSE.

THEY READ A BOOK ON DESIGNING HOUSES.

THEY REDESIGNED THEIR HOUSES AND LIVED HAPPILY EVER AFTER.

THE SAMPLE FAMILY

Let's meet Tom and Lois Sample and their daughter, Anna. I have invented them to provide a model of how a family with no architectural background might go about designing their own house following my step-by-step instructions and their own common sense.

We'll follow Tom, Lois, and their daughter throughout the book. At the end you should be able to look back and see how their needs, the uniqueness of their land, and their pocketbook dictated the final shape of their house.

TOM   LOIS   LUCY

Porches and landscaping are important parts of the design of the entry of any residence.

2 GETTING STARTED

After you've purchased your land, your very first task will be to set up a place to work, or your "architect's office."

It will be the center of activity for everything that relates to the design and the drawing of your new home.

These pages will show you how to set up an office that fits your needs. You'll be introduced to a group of simple drafting tools, materials, and methods, and provided with some instruction on how to use them.

This is the foundation of your work. Good luck!

SETTING UP YOUR OFFICE

Here are some simple ways of setting up a pleasant, well-lighted, well-ordered place to work that will organize all the little tools and pieces of information that otherwise might create an incomprehensible mess. Most of your supplies, including the lamp, can be purchased at an art or office supply store.

This page contains ideas for a very low-budget or minimal office. Its key advantage is that it is portable and can be stored away very easily.

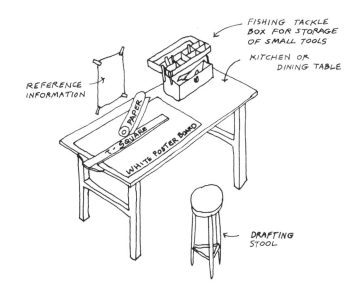

FISHING TACKLE BOX FOR STORAGE OF SMALL TOOLS

KITCHEN OR DINING TABLE

REFERENCE INFORMATION

PAPER

T-SQUARE

WHITE POSTER BOARD

DRAFTING STOOL

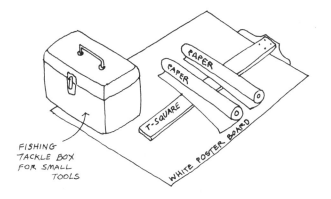

FISHING TACKLE BOX FOR SMALL TOOLS

T-SQUARE

PAPER

PAPER

WHITE POSTER BOARD

The opposite page shows how you might set up a more complete, permanent office. You may need more time and space (and therefore a larger office budget), but you may want to go this route if you want to work more efficiently.

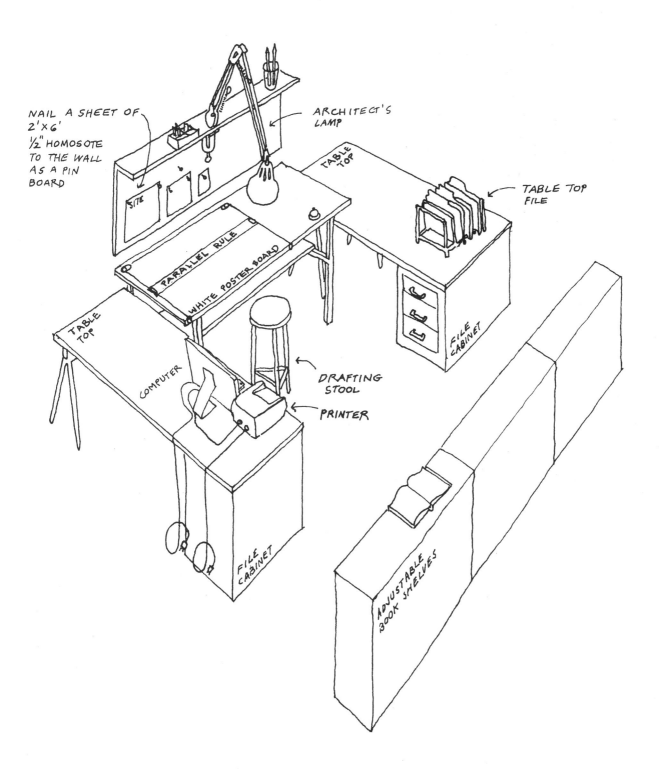

NAIL A SHEET OF 2'x6' ½" HOMOSOTE TO THE WALL AS A PIN BOARD

ARCHITECT'S LAMP

TABLE TOP

TABLE TOP FILE

SITE

PARALLEL RULE

WHITE POSTER BOARD

TABLE TOP

COMPUTER

FILE CABINET

DRAFTING STOOL

PRINTER

FILE CABINET

ADJUSTABLE BOOK SHELVES

BUYING YOUR TOOLS

Here is a shopping list with the minimum array of tools you'll need. Most are sold with various options as to quality and price. They are sold in drafting supply stores or through their catalogs.

Pick the tools and materials that fit your budget.

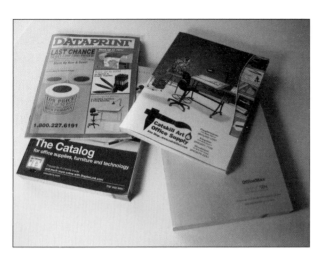

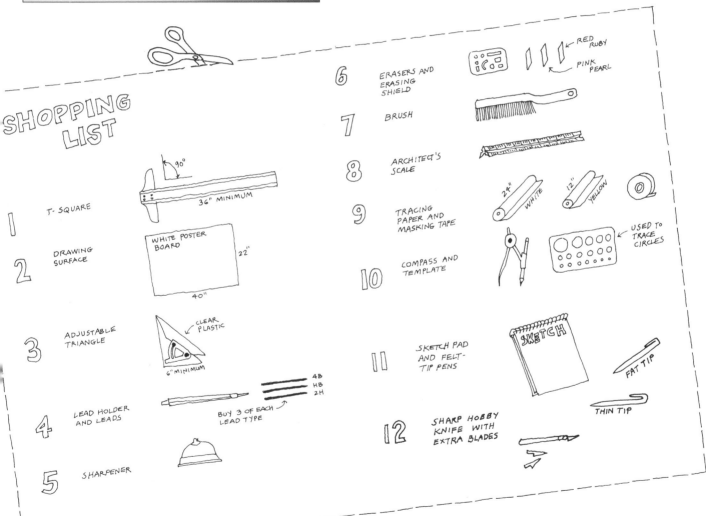

SHOPPING LIST

1. T-SQUARE — 90°, 36" MINIMUM

2. DRAWING SURFACE — WHITE POSTER BOARD, 22", 40"

3. ADJUSTABLE TRIANGLE — CLEAR PLASTIC, 6" MINIMUM

4. LEAD HOLDER AND LEADS — 4B, HB, 2H, BUY 3 OF EACH LEAD TYPE

5. SHARPENER

6. ERASERS AND ERASING SHIELD — RED RUBY, PINK PEARL

7. BRUSH

8. ARCHITECT'S SCALE

9. TRACING PAPER AND MASKING TAPE — 24" WHITE, 12" YELLOW

10. COMPASS AND TEMPLATE — USED TO TRACE CIRCLES

11. SKETCH PAD AND FELT-TIP PENS — SKETCH, FAT TIP, THIN TIP

12. SHARP HOBBY KNIFE WITH EXTRA BLADES

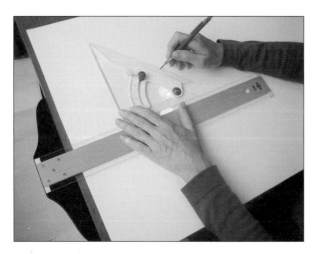

USING THE THREE BASIC TOOLS

The three basic tools for drafting are the parallel rule or T-square, the adjustable triangle, and the lead holder. Master their use and you're set.

The T-square rides along the left edge of the drawing board or table (right edge if you're left handed). It is used for drawing horizontal, parallel lines and as an edge base for the adjustable triangle. The parallel rule is used for the same purpose but is easier to use because you don't need to apply constant pressure on the outside edge to keep the rule steady and parallel. Its wire system keeps it constantly perpendicular to the left edge of the board.

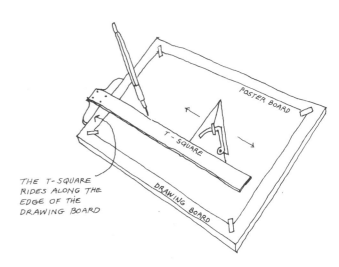

THE T-SQUARE
RIDES ALONG THE
EDGE OF THE
DRAWING BOARD

THE TRIANGLE
RIDES ALONG THE
TOP EDGE OF THE
PARALLEL RULE

THE PARALLEL
RULE STAYS
PARALLEL BECAUSE
IT RIDES ON A WIRE
TRACK SYSTEM.

Before you start, cover the drawing surface with a sheet of white poster board. This will make a bright, clean, smooth surface on which to draw and will keep the wooden table or board from getting dented by your pencil.

The adjustable triangle is a clear plastic tool with an adjustable leg, permitting you to draw lines at any angle.

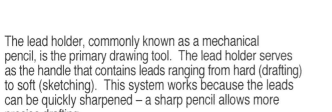

ADJUSTABLE LEG

TURN SCREW

ANGLE INDICATOR

VERTICAL AND 45° LINES

45° TO 90° LINES

0° TO 45° LINES

The lead holder, commonly known as a mechanical pencil, is the primary drawing tool. The lead holder serves as the handle that contains leads ranging from hard (drafting) to soft (sketching). This system works because the leads can be quickly sharpened – a sharp pencil allows more precise drafting.

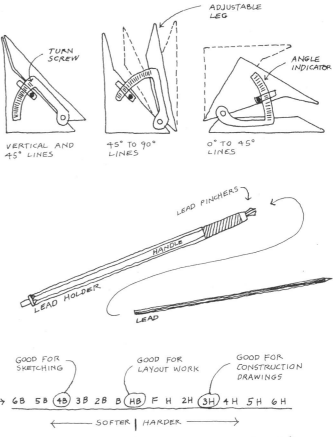

LEAD PINCHERS

HANDLE

LEAD HOLDER

LEAD

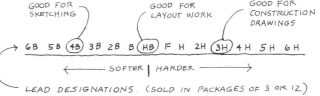

GOOD FOR SKETCHING

GOOD FOR LAYOUT WORK

GOOD FOR CONSTRUCTION DRAWINGS

6B 5B (4B) 3B 2B B (HB) F H 2H (3H) 4H 5H 6H

← SOFTER | HARDER →

LEAD DESIGNATIONS. (SOLD IN PACKAGES OF 3 OR 12)

USING THE SUPPORTING TOOLS

This section will show you how to use a few of the other drafting tools included on your shopping list . You'll need these supporting tools so that the primary tools can do their job.

You'll need a special sharpener for leads. It is designed to sharpen a lead quickly, necessary when you need to draw many fine lines in succession.

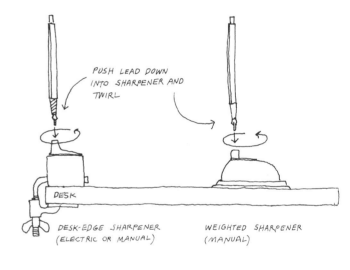

PUSH LEAD DOWN INTO SHARPENER AND TWIRL

DESK

DESK-EDGE SHARPENER (ELECTRIC OR MANUAL)

WEIGHTED SHARPENER (MANUAL)

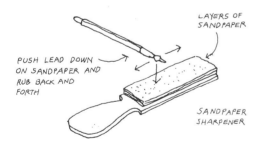

PUSH LEAD DOWN ON SANDPAPER AND RUB BACK AND FORTH

LAYERS OF SANDPAPER

SANDPAPER SHARPENER

There are two ways to draw circles. The first, and the easiest, is to use a template made for tracing circles. The second is with a compass, which is best for drawing the larger circles.

There are many other types of templates which can be used to trace various parts of your house design. Bathroom, fireplace, kitchen, and ellipse templates are most common. Put them on your shopping list if you think they'll help.

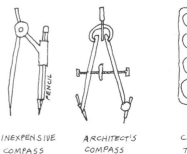

INEXPENSIVE COMPASS

ARCHITECT'S COMPASS

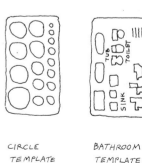

CIRCLE TEMPLATE

BATHROOM TEMPLATE

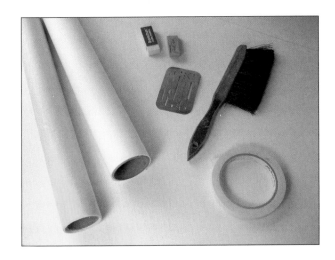

Using a fat eraser to correct mistakes when you are working on a finely detailed drawing is not fun. However, if you know how to use an erasing shield, you can erase a small area of your drawing while preserving the rest. The erasing shield is a thin, perforated sheet of metal used to limit the area being erased. The perforation is placed over the area to be erased while the metal sheet protects the rest.

Mistakes and changes requiring erasures are an inevitable part of the architect's work. Unfortunately, this is a part of the craft of drafting that you'll probably confront first.

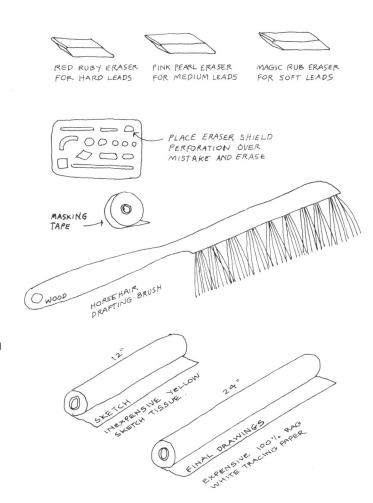

RED RUBY ERASER FOR HARD LEADS

PINK PEARL ERASER FOR MEDIUM LEADS

MAGIC RUB ERASER FOR SOFT LEADS

PLACE ERASER SHIELD PERFORATION OVER MISTAKE AND ERASE

MASKING TAPE

WOOD

HORSEHAIR DRAFTING BRUSH

12"

SKETCH INEXPENSIVE YELLOW SKETCH TISSUE

24"

FINAL DRAWINGS EXPENSIVE 100% RAG WHITE TRACING PAPER

The horsehair drafting brush is the tool used to remove eraser shavings from your drawing without smudging the pencil lines on the page.

You'll need two types of paper. The first is a roll of very inexpensive, thin yellow tracing tissue, often called canary paper, essential for sketching. The second is good quality, heavy white tracing paper for your final drawings.

Masking or drafting tape is used to hold the paper to the drawing surface without damaging the paper.

MAKING A SCRAPBOOK

A scrapbook is a compilation of ideas, primarily visual, that have inspired you and that you would like to use in the design of your home. The more time you can devote to it, the more exciting and complete your project will be.

The most popular insert in your scrapbook might be magazine tear sheets. There is an infinite amount of home - oriented glossies available, illustrating any style for almost any type of environment, both interior and exterior. Include clippings of any idea that you like, from furniture arrangement to a type of window or bath fixture. Remember, you're creating a guidebook for yourself.

Try to make your scrapbook as personal as you can. Notes, sketches, diagrams, pictures of your favorite furniture, collections, hobbies, and don't forget landscaping. A great photograph of an entryway or porch might be the perfect starting point for your future design work.

KEEP HANDY FOR NOTES, DIAGRAMS, AND SKETCHES TO INCLUDE IN YOUR SCRAPBOOK

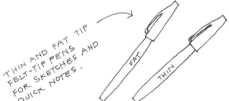

THIN AND FAT TIP FELT-TIP PENS FOR SKETCHES AND QUICK NOTES.

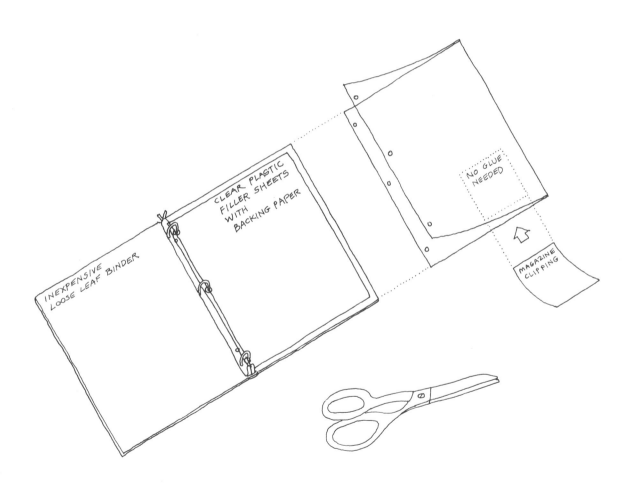

INEXPENSIVE
LOOSE LEAF BINDER

CLEAR PLASTIC
FILLER SHEETS
WITH
BACKING PAPER

NO GLUE
NEEDED

MAGAZINE
CLIPPING

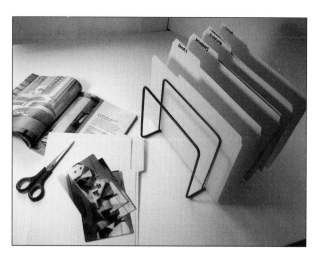

BUILDING A FILE

If you have a computer and can access the Internet, you'll find it very easy to research and compile information regarding all the products that you are likely to use in your new home.

Windows, doors, roofing, flooring, kitchen appliances and cabinets, bathroom fixtures, and tiles, are a few of the products available for online purchase from a wide variety of companies.

Print your computer-generated information and build a file. Ask each company to mail you a catalog. These brochures will give you many ideas about the best use of each product.

DEVELOP AN EASY ACCESS
FILE WITH MANILA FOLDERS
IN A FRAME

PRINTER

DIGITAL CAMERA
COLOR PRINTS FOR
YOUR FILE

If you don't have a computer or can't gain access to one, the Yellow Pages provide listings of companies that will send you product information to help build your file. All this research and free information is a vital part of your learning process – it will teach and inspire you as you design your perfect home.

The quickest method to record what you see is photography, especially now that the digital camera is so ubiquitous. As you travel, take pictures of houses, and details of houses or landscaping that interest and inspire you.

These photos are a valuable addition to your file. They will help you with the many design decisions you will need to make: color, types of windows and doors, landscape planning, roofing and siding materials, trimwork, and, most importantly, the style of your home.

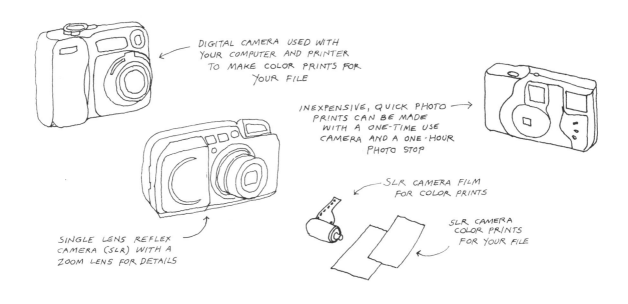

DIGITAL CAMERA USED WITH YOUR COMPUTER AND PRINTER TO MAKE COLOR PRINTS FOR YOUR FILE

INEXPENSIVE, QUICK PHOTO PRINTS CAN BE MADE WITH A ONE-TIME USE CAMERA AND A ONE-HOUR PHOTO STOP

SINGLE LENS REFLEX CAMERA (SLR) WITH A ZOOM LENS FOR DETAILS

SLR CAMERA FILM FOR COLOR PRINTS

SLR CAMERA COLOR PRINTS FOR YOUR FILE

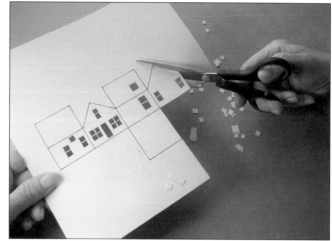

BUILDING A STUDY MODEL

Study models are used to help you understand your design in three dimensions. They are easier to build than you might think and are a critical tool for exploring shape and understanding how the light particular to your site will affect your design.

Heavy-weight paper, often called smooth finish Bristol Board, can be cut with scissors or a sharp hobby knife. Using light pressure on your hobby knife, score the edges. Cut the windows before folding and glueing to produce a cleaner edge.

Use the cut-out on the opposite page to start practicing your model-building. Have patience, build a few simple models, cut a few extra windows and glue lightly. It's easy!

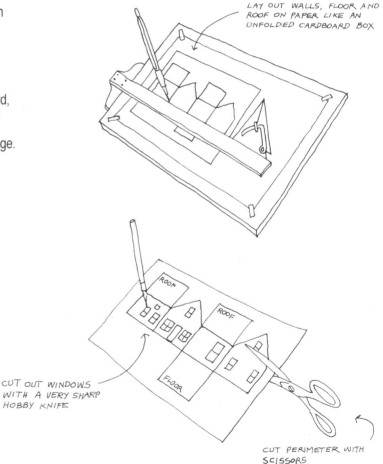

LAY OUT WALLS, FLOOR AND ROOF ON PAPER LIKE AN UNFOLDED CARDBOARD BOX

CUT OUT WINDOWS WITH A VERY SHARP HOBBY KNIFE

CUT PERIMETER WITH SCISSORS

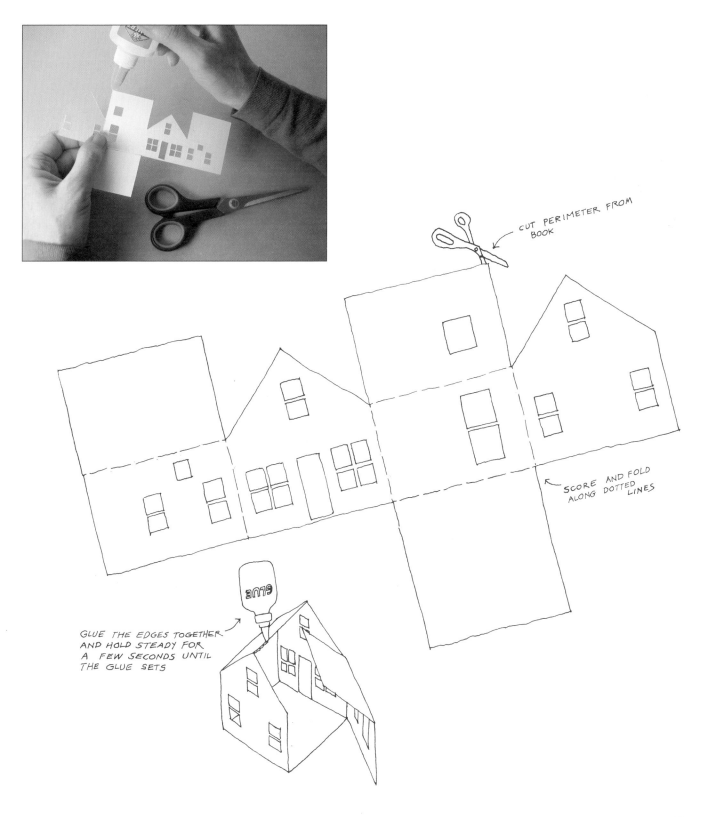

CUT PERIMETER FROM BOOK

SCORE AND FOLD ALONG DOTTED LINES

GLUE

GLUE THE EDGES TOGETHER AND HOLD STEADY FOR A FEW SECONDS UNTIL THE GLUE SETS

29

USING A SCALE

Architects use a ruler or "scale," as a tool to reduce objects to a size that will fit on a drawing. A common scale is 1/4" = 1'-0", or one quarter of an inch is equal to one foot. In other words, a 12-foot-long wall would be drawn as 12 quarters of an inch and would appear on your drawing as three inches long. This scale reduces the wall by 48 times.

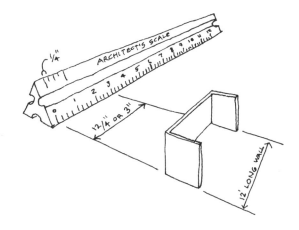

If you decide that the three-inch line is too small and hard to work with, you might choose a larger scale of one half-inch equals one foot. This would reduce the 12-foot wall to twelve halves of an inch and appear on your drawing as 6 inches long. This reduces the wall by 24 times.

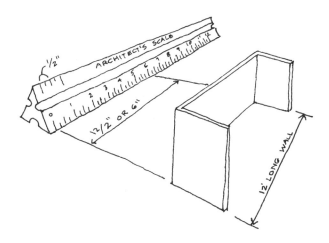

There are 11 different scales on the architect's ruler with which you can experiment to arrive at one that will make it possible to fit your drawing on the page.

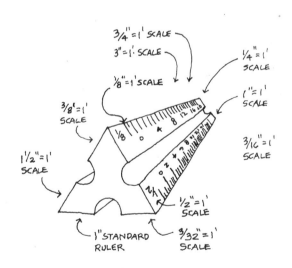

3/4" = 1' SCALE
3" = 1' SCALE
1/8" = 1' SCALE
1/4" = 1' SCALE
1" = 1' SCALE
3/8" = 1' SCALE
3/16" = 1' SCALE
1 1/2" = 1' SCALE
1/2" = 1' SCALE
1" STANDARD RULER
3/32" = 1' SCALE

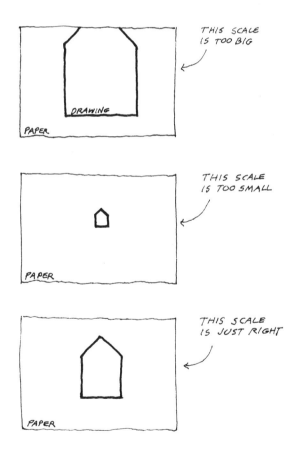

THIS SCALE IS TOO BIG

DRAWING
PAPER

THIS SCALE IS TOO SMALL

PAPER

THIS SCALE IS JUST RIGHT

PAPER

Now that you've made an office and set up your architect's tools, it's time to start.

You must practice with each tool until you feel comfortable using it. If you feel you cannot draw well, don't worry – you are teaching yourself a technical procedure, not an artistic one.

Practice, practice, practice. You'll see – it's easy!

Colored volumes can fit together to create a home that adjusts to your site.

3 DRAWING YOUR SITE

Spend a day at your site with a pencil and yellow tracing paper, sketching the location of property lines, ground slope, roads, utility locations, existing buildings (including neighbors), trees, streams, rocks, and other natural features. This information can be used to make a more refined drawing later.

Site conditions play a key role in determining the shape of your house. Be diligent and record as many as possible. The more you draw, the more you discover, the better your design, the richer the final result – in that order.

DRAWING YOUR MAN-MADE FEATURES

To begin to study your site, you'll need to get used to the idea that you're looking down on your land from high above. The drawing that you are making is often called a "bird's eye view."

Here are a few of the most important man-made features that you need to locate on your drawing.

Property lines are marked on a survey map – usually obtained from the seller of your land.

Views are often man-made by cutting trees or brush. It will be best to visit your land when the leaves are off the trees to see the views you want. Otherwise, you'll have to use your imagination.

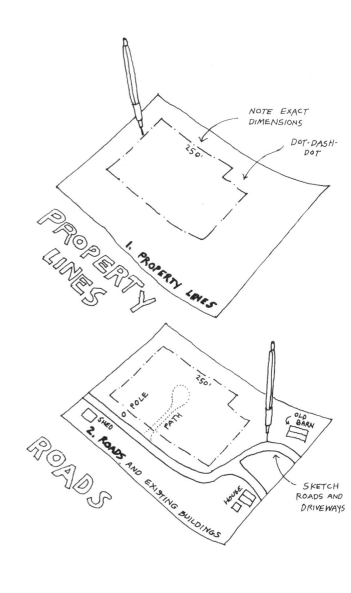

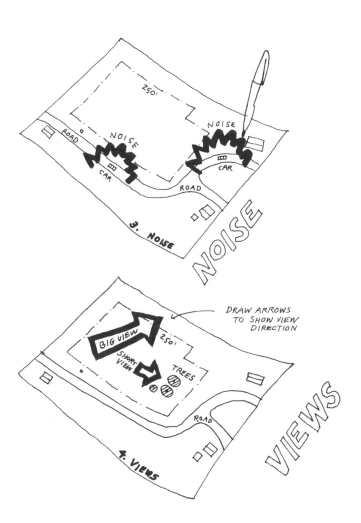

3. NOISE

NOISE

4. VIEWS

VIEWS

DRAW ARROWS
TO SHOW VIEW
DIRECTION

BIG VIEW

SHORT VIEW

TREES

250'

ROAD

DRAWING YOUR NATURAL FEATURES

Here are a few of the most important natural features that you need to locate on your drawing. If it is impossible to gather this information by camping on your land, talk to neighbors or others who might be familiar with your site conditions.

Contours can be estimated by judging your slopes when you walk your land. If your site is complex or you want to be very accurate, you might ask the surveyor to include them on your site survey.

You're now ready to make a neat, accurate drawing of your site conditions.

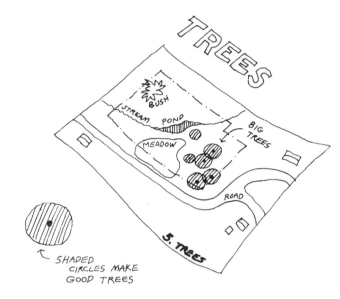

SHADED CIRCLES MAKE GOOD TREES

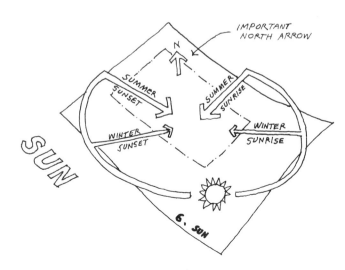

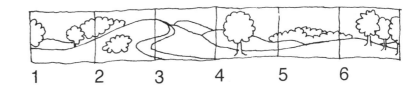

1   2   3   4   5   6

A PANORAMIC PHOTOGRAPH
OF YOUR SITE CAN BE MADE
BY ROTATING YOUR CAMERA
SO THAT A SECOND VIEW
BEGINS WHERE THE FIRST
ONE ENDED, AND SO
ON, UNTIL YOU
HAVE A
CONTINUOUS
360° RECORDING.

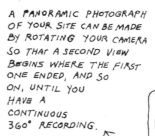

ROTATE CAMERA

1

2

3

4

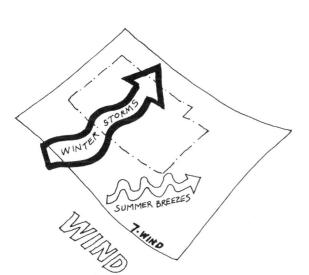

WINTER STORMS

SUMMER BREEZES

WIND

7. WIND

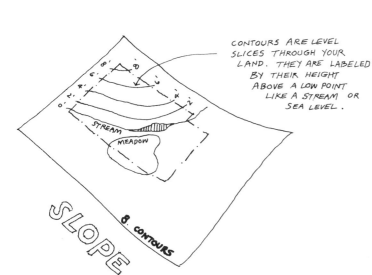

8'   8
6
4
2
0

STREAM

MEADOW

SLOPE

8. CONTOURS

CONTOURS ARE LEVEL
SLICES THROUGH YOUR
LAND. THEY ARE LABELED
BY THEIR HEIGHT
ABOVE A LOW POINT
LIKE A STREAM OR
SEA LEVEL.

COMPLETING YOUR SITE DRAWING

Now that you've gathered all this information about your land and you've set up your new office, it's time for your site drawing.

It is really just a collection of symbols illustrating all the conditions of your land. These conditions and their symbols were discussed on the preceding four pages.

Begin with the four man-made features and finish with the four natural features. Of course, add any other information you think necessary.

Here is how your final site drawing might look.

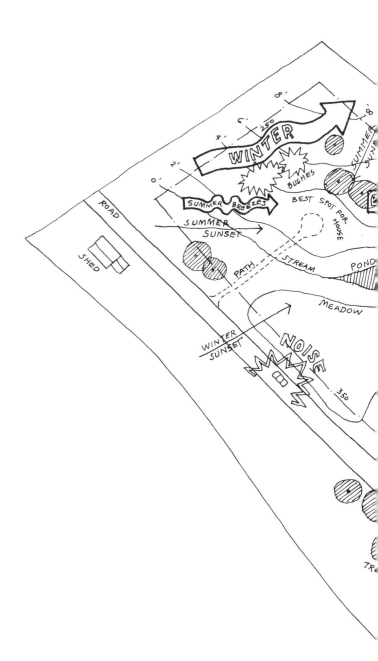

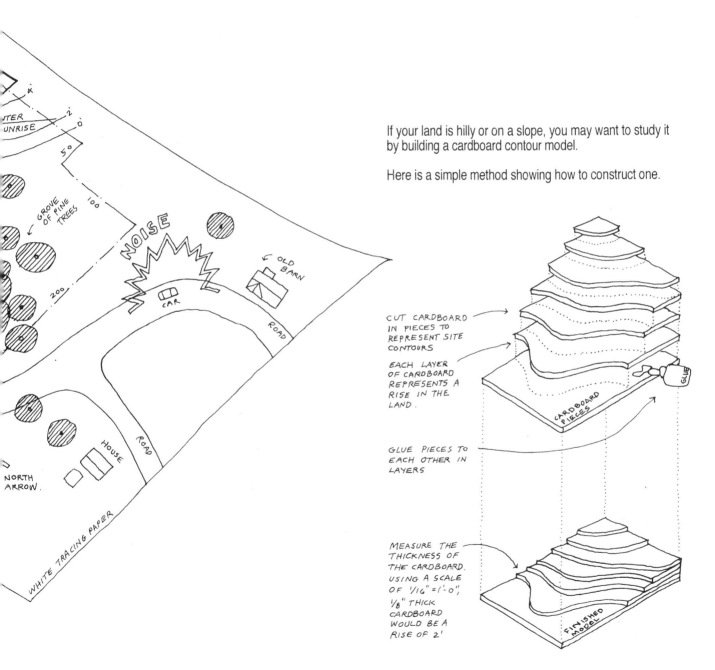

If your land is hilly or on a slope, you may want to study it by building a cardboard contour model.

Here is a simple method showing how to construct one.

CUT CARDBOARD IN PIECES TO REPRESENT SITE CONTOURS

EACH LAYER OF CARDBOARD REPRESENTS A RISE IN THE LAND.

GLUE PIECES TO EACH OTHER IN LAYERS

MEASURE THE THICKNESS OF THE CARDBOARD. USING A SCALE OF 1/16" = 1'-0", 1/8" THICK CARDBOARD WOULD BE A RISE OF 2'

CARDBOARD PIECES

GLUE

FINISHED MODEL

ITER
UNRISE

4'
2'
0'
50
GROVE OF PINE TREES
100
200
NOISE
CAR
OLD BARN
ROAD
ROAD
HOUSE
NORTH ARROW.
WHITE TRACING PAPER

Color can be used to express various shapes of your design, thereby giving it more charm and interest.

4 MAKING A WISH LIST

A typical wish list is one that includes a compilation of
room requirements with size and function, plus a listing of
your ideas for each room. A better, more complete list
would add your sketches, notes, magazine clippings,
a set of rules that you don't wish to break, and, of course,
your dreams.

A scrapbook, as discussed on page 24, is a necessity.
Don't hesitate to load it up with all your thoughts. It will make
an excellent "program" for all your future design work.

OBSERVING HOUSES

As you travel, how you see and what you observe can be very important in your development as a house designer. You can teach yourself to be focused and aware as you look at one of your favorite houses.

A quick, easy first step to analyzing any house is to visually break it down into its primary volumes. This can teach you how the building's designer used geometric building-block-like shapes to relate to the site, to conform to a particular architectural style, to adjust to the owner's "program,"or simply to expand the building.

Shown here are two examples of this idea. With some practice you should be able to see any house as a single, simple volume or as a collection of a variety of shapes, even as you speed by them in your car.

Try to understand why you like the house and why you don't. There are many field guides to house styles that can help you identify a particular house style you may prefer.

Then try to sketch or photograph any details that you like, for example, porches, entryways, windows, doors, and chimneys.

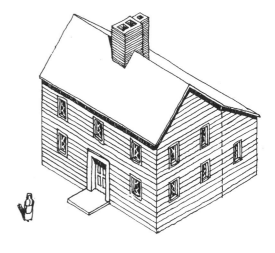

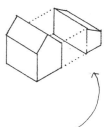

A SIMPLE NEW ENGLAND FARMHOUSE IS CHANGED INTO A "SALTBOX" WITH THE ADDITION OF A SECOND VOLUME

Even the most architecturally complex mansion can be understood when its massing is deconstructed into geometric shapes.

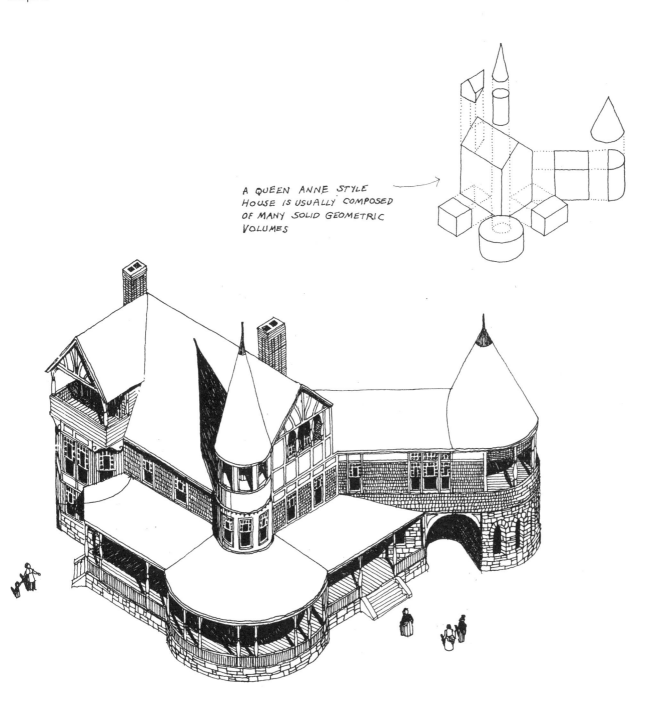

A QUEEN ANNE STYLE HOUSE IS USUALLY COMPOSED OF MANY SOLID GEOMETRIC VOLUMES

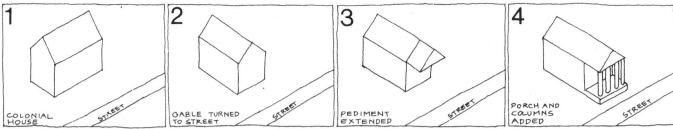

1	2	3	4
COLONIAL HOUSE — STREET	GABLE TURNED TO STREET — STREET	PEDIMENT EXTENDED — STREET	PORCH AND COLUMNS ADDED — STREET

CONVERTING A COLONIAL HOUSE DESIGN INTO A GREEK REVIVAL HOUSE DESIGN

Every building is first designed as a single volume or a collection of volumes. Architects think of them as three-dimensional diagrams that they can easily manipulate during the design process.

Shown on these two pages are a few more examples of houses as volumetric parts.

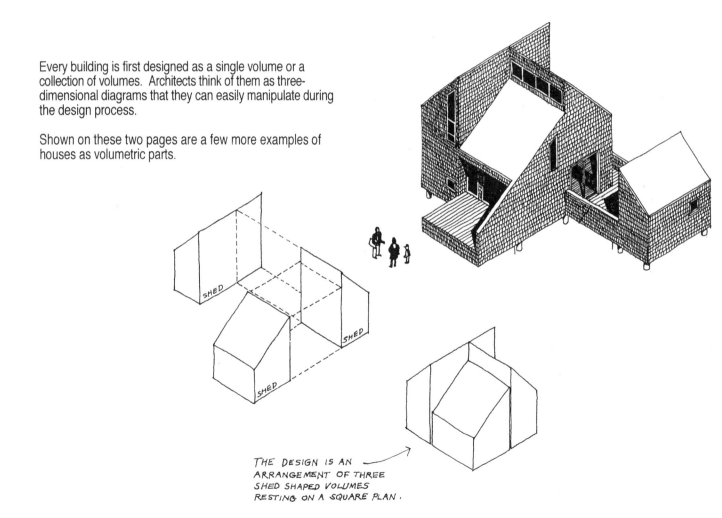

THE DESIGN IS AN ARRANGEMENT OF THREE SHED SHAPED VOLUMES RESTING ON A SQUARE PLAN.

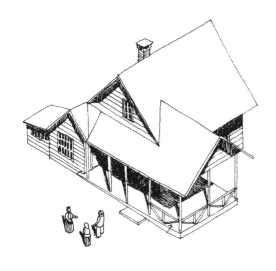

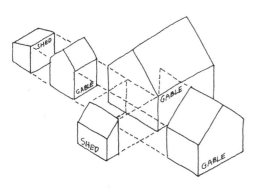

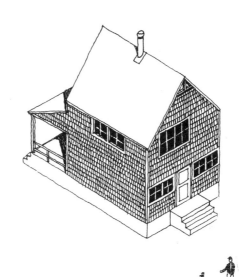

CONCAVE MANSARD ROOF!

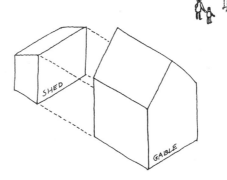

Different roofs are used to manipulate the shape of the volume.

1 FLAT ROOF   2 GABLE ROOF   3 SHED ROOF   4 HIPPED ROOF   5 HALF-HIPPED ROOF   6 GAMBREL ROOF   7 STRAIGHT MANSARD ROOF   8 CONCAVE MANSARD ROOF   9 CONVEX MANSARD ROOF   10 PYRAMIDAL ROOF   11 RAINBOW ROOF   12 BUTTERFLY ROOF

SKETCHING HOUSES

Sketching, or drawing, is one of the most important skills to develop because it is the simplest form of visual communication. The best way to learn how to do it is to just do it. Sketching the exterior, interior, or details of any building can instantly give you an understanding of how it is built, what materials are used, what style it is, the reasons for its shape, how it uses natural light, and whether it is elegant or funky. In short, sketching is an excellent educational exercise.

Take time to look carefully at what you are sketching. How is each element related to the others? Do the windows line up? If not, why? Where are the chimneys and why are they there? Is there fancy detailing around the doors and windows? What type of windows are used? Note the materials that are used on the exterior and interior of the house.

You need not always do complete drawings. Often a small detail sketch, perhaps with a note, will record just what you want to remember.

This information will help you as you make your wish list and begin to develop a design.

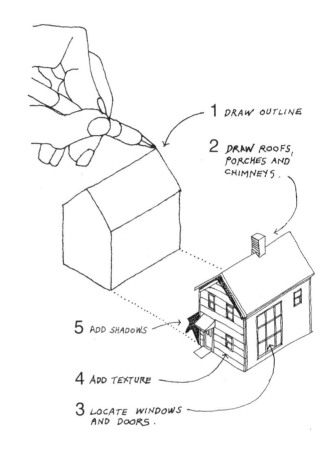

1 DRAW OUTLINE

2 DRAW ROOFS, PORCHES AND CHIMNEYS.

5 ADD SHADOWS

4 ADD TEXTURE

3 LOCATE WINDOWS AND DOORS.

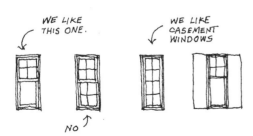

WE LIKE THIS ONE.

WE LIKE CASEMENT WINDOWS

NO

TOM! COME LOOK AT THESE SHUTTERS.

When you are in a room that you like, it's a good idea to make a quick sketch of it, including approximate dimensions.

Here are five ways to record a room.

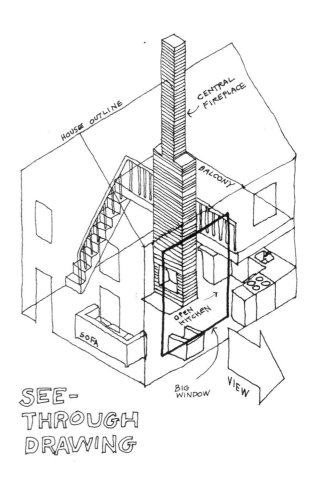

SEE-THROUGH DRAWING

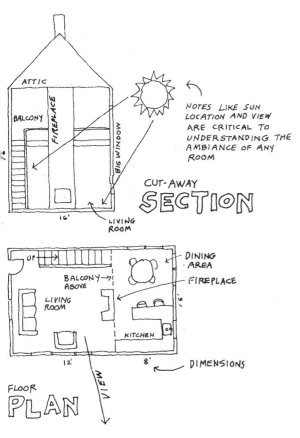

NOTES LIKE SUN LOCATION AND VIEW ARE CRITICAL TO UNDERSTANDING THE AMBIANCE OF ANY ROOM

CUT-AWAY SECTION

FLOOR PLAN

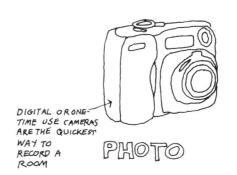

DIGITAL OR ONE-TIME USE CAMERAS ARE THE QUICKEST WAY TO RECORD A ROOM

PHOTO

When you see an inside space that you like, ask yourself why you like it. Study what is going on in the room: How does the light enter? Does it reflect off of anything? How are color and texture used? How does the space feel – open or intimate – and why? Try asking yourself these questions as you look. Then, photograph/sketch/note your thoughts and add them to that great scrapbook you've started.

On the opposite page are two very small houses whose interior space, including furnishings, is shown with a see-through drawing – an excellent method to use for cataloging interiors.

Your personal notations will remind you at a later date what you liked or disliked about the space.

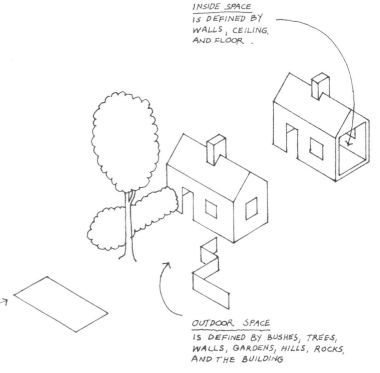

INSIDE SPACE
IS DEFINED BY
WALLS, CEILING,
AND FLOOR.

SPACE

IS AN ARCHITECT'S
WORD

AREA
IS NOT A SPACE

OUTDOOR SPACE
IS DEFINED BY BUSHES, TREES,
WALLS, GARDENS, HILLS, ROCKS,
AND THE BUILDING

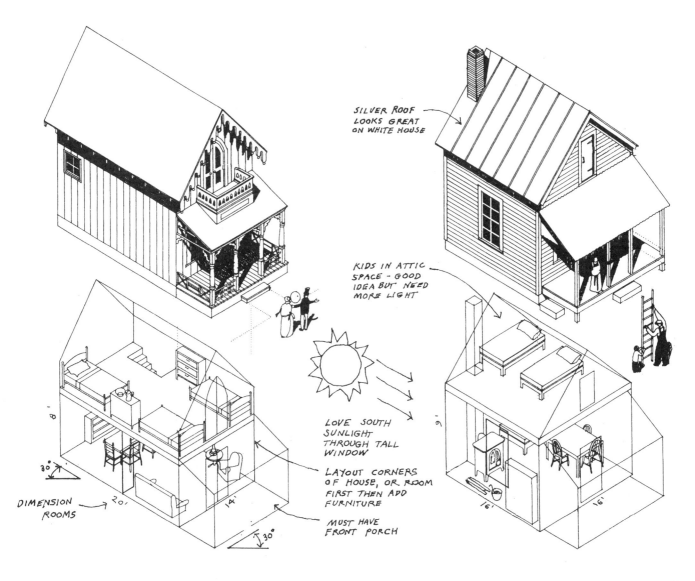

SILVER ROOF
LOOKS GREAT
ON WHITE HOUSE

KIDS IN ATTIC
SPACE - GOOD
IDEA BUT NEED
MORE LIGHT

LOVE SOUTH
SUNLIGHT
THROUGH TALL
WINDOW

LAYOUT CORNERS
OF HOUSE, OR ROOM
FIRST THEN ADD
FURNITURE

MUST HAVE
FRONT PORCH

DIMENSION
ROOMS

20'

14'

8'

30°

30°

9'

16'

16'

LISTING YOUR
GENERAL REQUIREMENTS

A wish list is really a scrapbook filled with ideas of what you think should be included in your home design. In addition to your observations, notes, and sketches (discussed on the previous pages), you should provide a written description of all your requirements, both general and specific, for the interior and exterior of your home. Architects often call this list a "program."

The first list you'll need is a general requirements wish list consisting of ideas about the home as a whole. For example, how does it look from the outside or how should it feel on the inside? How should the design relate to the group of people living there? How large is the group? Are there any special family activities that need to be considered, for example, large dinner parties, singing around the piano, or outdoor play spaces? It's up to you and your family to develop your own list of general requirements – your program – based on your lives together as a unit.

On the opposite page is a typical general requirements wish list.

WISH LIST

COST	COST TO BUILD PER SQUARE FOOT X OUR PROJECTED SQUARE FOOTAGE = COST NEED TO SET A MAXIMUM COST ·
STYLE	SIMPLE WHITE NEW ENGLAND FARMHOUSE WITH GENEROUS ENTRY SLOPE ROOFS NICE WINDOW TRIM DECK
LIGHT	EVERY ROOM EXCEPT THE BEDROOMS MUST HAVE BRIGHT DIRECT SUNLIGHT SKYLIGHTS NOT NECESSARY
INTERIORS	HIGH LIVING ROOM CEILING · MAYBE 10' WHITE WALLS & TRIMWORK WOOD FLOORS NATURAL WOOD DOORS
GARDENS	AROUND HOUSE + ENTRY KITCHEN GARDEN IF POSSIBLE
KITCHEN · DINING	ONE SPACE · EFFICIENT - NOT TOO SMALL WHITE VIEW WHILE DISHWASHING BIG VIEWS FOR DINING - FOR 10 PEOPLE (MAX·)
YARD	CROQUET, BADMINTON YARD · LOVE TO CUT GRASS TRY TO SURROUND GARDEN WITH LAWN NEED SHADY AREA
LAUNDRY	PART OF KITCHEN · CAN BE STACKED WASHER/ DRYER
RECYCLING	CAN BE PART OF PANTRY - LAUNDRY AREA GARBAGE NEAR SINK
GREEN	SUPER INSULATED HOUSE SOLAR HOT WATER HEATER WOOD - BURNING STOVE TRIPLE GLAZED WINDOWS GREEN MATERIALS HIGH - EFFICIENT HEAT
STORAGE	WE ARE NOT COLLECTORS SHELVES IN ALL CLOTHES CLOSETS ENTRY CLOSET OUTDOOR STORAGE
HEAT	GEO - THERMAL HEAT + AC IF WE CAN AFFORD IT · IF NOT · HIGH EFFICIENCY GAS NEED TO TALK TO INSTALLERS
PORCH DECK	NICE FRONT ENTRY COVERED PORCH DECK FOR SUN & DINING
FIREPLACE	FIREPLACE WILL BREAK BUDGET GLASS - FRONT WOODBURNING STOVE - OK IN LIVING ROOM
SLEEPING	SLEEPING ROOMS CAN BE VERY SMALL - FOR SLEEPING + DRESSING MUST HAVE FRESH AIR
VIEWS	LIVING ROOM + DINING ROOM MUST HAVE GOOD VIEWS WITH BIG WINDOWS BRING OUTSIDE - IN

TOM! WE FORGOT THE COMPUTER ·

LISTING YOUR
ROOM REQUIREMENTS

The most specific part of your scrapbook program is a room requirement wish list. This is a simple chart of all the predicted rooms or spaces in the house with as many descriptive categories as you feel are necessary.

Before you and your family develop your list, here are some ideas you may want to consider that will help you design a more efficient home. Remember, a smaller house is less expensive to build, heat, and cool. Taxes are less and maintenance is minimized. The greener the home, the better for all.

1. Consider making the kitchen, dining room, and living room a single combined space, each borrowing from the other.

2. Maximize the window use on one major wall. Take advantage of the sun and a great view. Bring the outside to the inside. When rooms have good natural lighting, they don't seem small.

3. Raise the ceiling in part of the house, perhaps the living room or dining room. This can make the whole interior feel larger.

4. Level changes can be used to separate one space from another. For example, the living room floor can be dropped two steps, or 16", below the other floors, with this level change used for seating. It will feel like a different room without needing walls.

5. Include a large, comfortable entryway. Try to design it so that a view is visible, making it feel big and exciting. You don't want to walk into a home that feels inconvenient and tight at its entry.

6. Build in as much furniture as possible to save space.

7. If possible eliminate hallways. They waste space.

8. Design inexpensive porches, patios, and decks as necessary accessories to your home. Easy access to the outdoors makes your house work better and seem larger.

9. Design outdoor rooms with shrubs, lawns, trees, fences, patios, rock outcroppings, and walls with easy visual access to your indoor rooms. The more you incorporate the outdoors, the more you can reduce the size of your house.

10. Use residual spaces (transition areas not given over to a specific function) for small offices, closets, computer stations, entertainment centers, recycling areas, and miscellaneous storage units. In short, make every square inch of space in your design, every nook and cranny, work for you.

On the opposite page is a typical room requirements wish list.

ROOM REQUIREMENTS

WISH LIST

ROOM NAME	WHO USES	APPROX. SIZE	SQ. FT.	NATURAL LIGHT	NEXT TO	CHARACTER	NOTES
LIVING	ALL	12×16	192	BRIGHT	DINING ENTRY	LIGHT AIRY	HIGH CEILING BIG VIEW WHITE WALLS WOOD FLOOR
DINING	ALL	12×10	120	BRIGHT	KITCHEN LIVING	LIGHT VIEW	SAME AS LIVING BUT 8' CEILING OPENS TO DECK
KITCHEN	TOM LOIS	12×8	96	BRIGHT	DINING PANTRY	BRIGHT	WHITE CABINETS VIEW GRANITE TOPS S.S. APPLIANCES
LAUNDRY PANTRY	TOM LOIS	3×6	18	DOESN'T MATTER	KITCHEN	UTILITY	STACKED WASHER·DRYER MANY SHELVES
½ BATH	ALL	4×5	20	DOESN'T MATTER	ENTRY	UTILITY	2 FIXTURES NICE WALLPAPER
ENTRY	ALL	8×10	80	SUBDUED SOFT	LIVING ROOM	DOWN PLAY	INCLUDES COAT CLOSET OPEN VIEW OF HOUSE
MASTER BEDROOM	TOM LOIS	12×14	168	DARK SOFT	MASTER BATH	NATURAL WOOD	CARPET WOOD WALLS DRESSING AREA VIEW
BEDROOM	ANNA	12×12	144	DARK SOFT	BATH	NATURAL WOOD	CLOTHES CLOSET TWIN BEDS HOMEWORK AREA
GUEST BEDROOM	PARENTS FRIENDS	11×12	132	DARK SOFT	BATH	NATURAL WOOD	CLOSET MIGHT DOUBLE AS OFFICE
MASTER BATH	TOM LOIS	6×9	54	BRIGHT	M. BEDROOM	CLEAN WHITE	ALL WHITE WALLS + FIXTURES TILED FLOOR + SHOWER
BATH	GUESTS	5×8	40	BRIGHT	G. BEDROOM	CLEAN WHITE	ALL WHITE WALLS + FIXTURES WHITE TILE FLOOR
OFFICE	TOM LOIS	11×10	110	BRIGHT	ENTRY	NO GLARE	COMPUTER· FILES CARPET BIG WORK TABLE
COMPUTER	ALL	3×6	18	DARK	LIVING	DARK	FILE CABINETS OFFICE PRINTER

TOTAL = 1192

238 ← ADD 20% MORE SQUARE FEET FOR CIRCULATION AND MISCELLANEOUS NEEDS

1430 ← TOTAL PROJECTED HOUSE DESIGN SQUARE FEET - NOT INCLUDING PORCHES + DECKS.

WOULDN'T IT BE GREAT IF ALL OUR WISHES CAME TRUE?

COMPLETING YOUR
WISH-LIST SCRAPBOOK

Your scrapbook, as noted before, is your program for the design
of your house. It contains all your likes and dislikes, your favorite
images, and your dreams for every part of your home, both interior
and exterior.

Wrapping up this part of your project might take some time but, as
you will see, it will serve you well as your design proceeds.

REALLY LIKE WOOD
SHINGLES AND
SHUTTERS

DOUBLE DOORS TO
SECOND FLOOR BALCONY.
WOULD BE NICE

LOVE THIS FRONT PORCH
WITH ORNAMENTAL
RAILINGS

MUST HAVE ENGLISH
FLOWER GARDEN

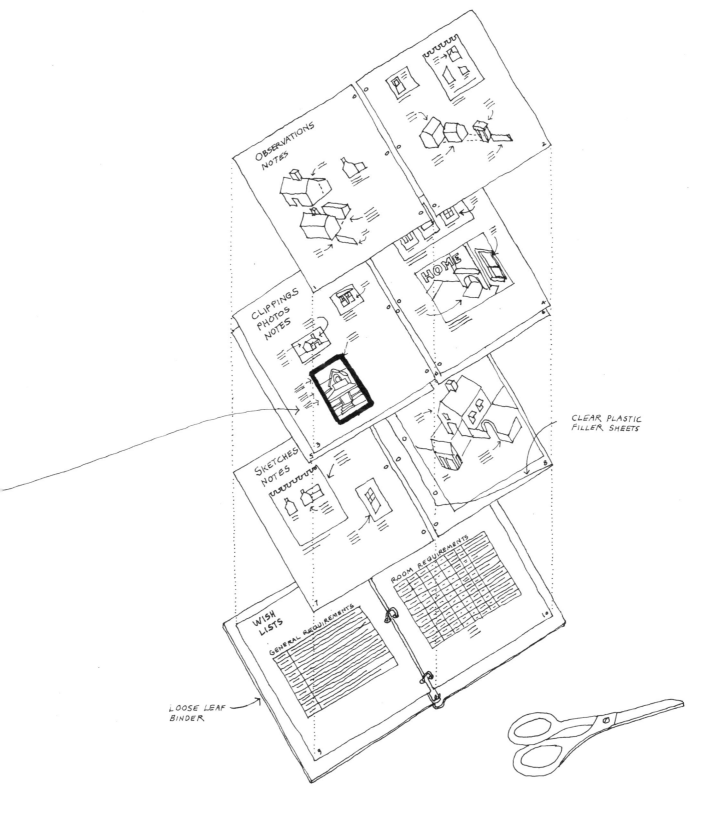

OBSERVATIONS
NOTES

CLIPPINGS
PHOTOS
NOTES

HOME

SKETCHES
NOTES

WISH
LISTS

GENERAL REQUIREMENTS

ROOM REQUIREMENTS

CLEAR PLASTIC
FILLER SHEETS

LOOSE LEAF
BINDER

Keep the shapes of your design as simple as possible. These modern shed-like volumes open to a wonderful streamside view.

5 DESIGNING

Designing is a process that involves collecting information, evaluating that information, and then decision-making based on your evaluation. You'll find that you will be constantly re-thinking your design as new ideas occur.

In this chapter I will demonstrate how to begin your design by imagining blobs of space (bubbles) floating around your site and landing on the perfect spot. Your wish lists will be your primary guide, but I will also provide some key site planning-principals to integrate with your thinking.

When you are comfortable with the layout of your bubbles, we'll graduate to imagining the bubbles as real rooms on your site. We'll use sketches to change the bubbles into "ideal" rooms (your perfect idea of a bedroom, etc.) and models to check your work.

Finally, I'll show you how to combine your ideal rooms to start making your house. This will take patience and careful evaluation, but you will find that this is the fun part of designing your own home.

USING BUBBLE DIAGRAMS

Now that you've completed your wish list, you are ready to begin working with a design technique that is used by every architect – bubble diagrams.

The method is to quickly represent interior spaces with amorphous blob-like shapes so that they can be studied and discussed. This method is an excellent way to locate the primary spaces of a building on a site and to study how these spaces relate to one another.

Give the bubbles names from your room requirement wish list and begin arranging them on your site in their most optimum location. Begin with your entry and let the building grow like a flower. Think about the sun, wind, noise, views, trees, and other forces acting on each bubble on your site.

Explore different possibilities. You may want to give each function a color to further distinguish the rooms in your diagram. For example, eating could be yellow, sleeping could be blue, and so on. Another idea is to cut out paper discs and move them around your site drawing.

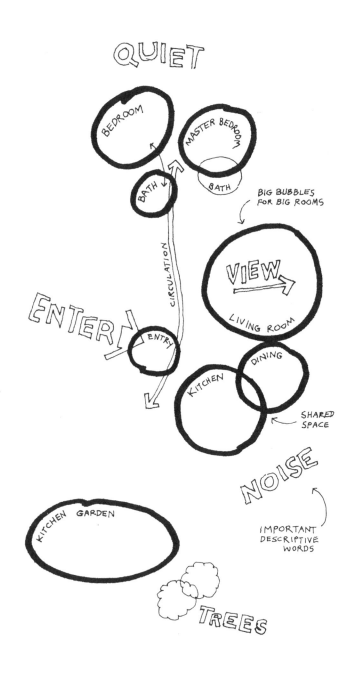

Here are some possible bubble arrangements:

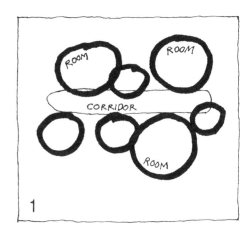

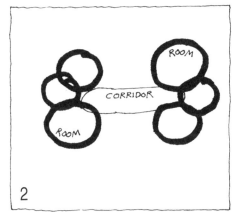

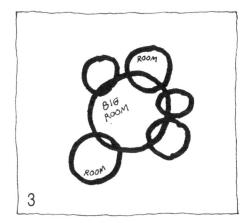

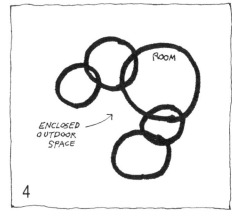

1 *Rooms opening off of a corridor.* This is a traditional way of organizing rooms. The drawback is that it wastes space because the corridor cannot be used for other functions.

2 *Rooms at opposite ends of a corridor.* This plan is used to achieve a separation, perhaps between quiet and noisy areas.

3 *Rooms opening off of a large communal room.* This arrangement offers less privacy than others, but it is a more efficient use of space since there are no corridors.

4 *Rooms used to enclose space.* Good for visual privacy, or to block winds or gather breezes.

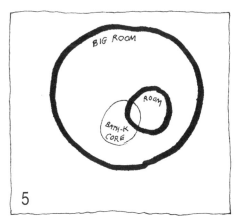

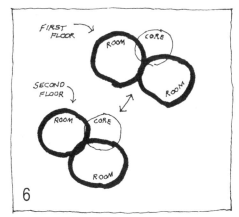

5 *Rooms within a room.* For example, a kitchen and bathroom core might sit in the center of a large room which would provide living, dining, and sleeping space.

6 *Rooms above rooms.* This diagram would create a two-story house. Think about where the stairs would be. Consider upper spaces that open to rooms below.

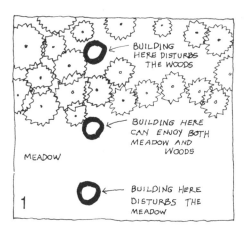

BUBBLE DIAGRAMMING ON YOUR SITE

Once you feel comfortable sketching room relationships using bubbles, begin to design with them on your site drawing. Here are some basic site-planning principles that you will want to keep in mind as you work.

1   *Land use.* Locate your home at the edge of a meadow or woods so as not to disturb either.

2   *Drainage.* Locate your home in a dry area that drains well.

3   *View.* Locate the windows of your home to take advantage of both the long and short views of your site.

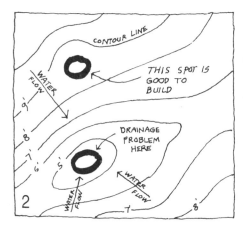

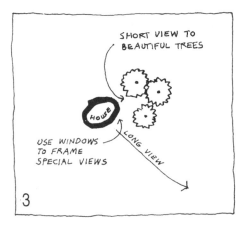

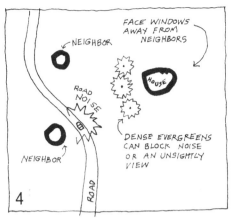

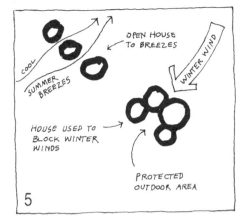

4 *Privacy.* Consider noise and neighbors.

5 *Wind.* Consider the direction of summer breezes and winter winds.

6 *Sun.* Consider how the sun moves through your site during the winter and summer days.

7 *Morning light.* Make sure to give rooms like the kitchen, breakfast area, and bathrooms good morning light.

8 *North light.* Consider facing windows north in rooms that you don't want glare, like an artist's studio.

9 *Entry.* Consider the entrance to your site from the public road. Make your driveway as dramatic and efficient as possible.

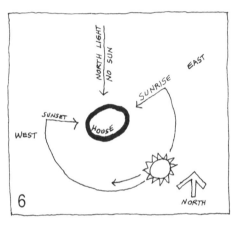

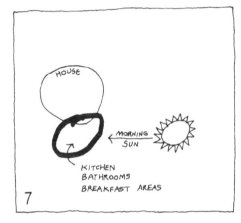

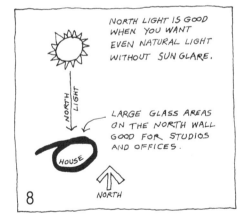

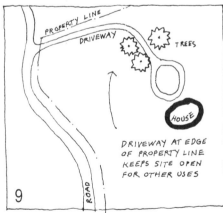

Now that you have drawn your site plan (Chapter 3), written your wish list, and have a basic understanding of the principles of bubble diagramming, you'll need to combine that information by designing with bubbles over your site. Use yellow tracing paper and sketch away until you have a bubble arrangement that you like.

To give you an idea about how this might work, I'll show you how Tom and Lois Sample diagrammed their home ideas.

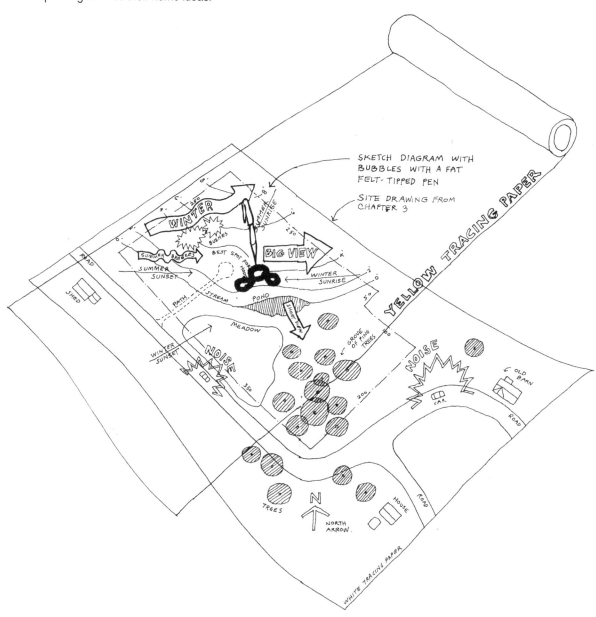

Tom and Lois decide that they want their house with every major room opening up to a deck with a view of their pond. They draw the pond part of their site drawing on yellow tracing paper and start with the bubble arrangement shown here.

This first spot was chosen because it has a south orientation to the pond, allowing a view of the pond, the pine tree grove beyond, and sun all day.

The bubbles show a room arrangement of *rooms opening off of a corridor* with the bedrooms getting early morning light and the living room getting late afternoon light. The kitchen, bathroom, and study get north light. The major rooms get a wonderful orientation to a deck that overlooks the pond and the pine grove.

The driveway is strategically located and will make a nice entry to the home. The existing path can still be used for walks to town.

The negative aspects of this arrangement are that it does not take advantage of the big view to the east and the bedrooms are too close to the noise and pollution of the road.

They decide to keep diagramming. They are determined to find a way to open the house to that big view and to make the bedrooms more quiet.

The second spot was chosen because Lois thought it would be wonderful to enter the house by way of a bridge over the stream. She also liked the idea of being closer to the pine grove. Tom liked the living room facing the big view to the east, and they both felt that the bedrooms would be more quiet in this new location.

They decided to build an earth berm near the public road to combat the traffic noise. They were happy with the relationship of the dining room to the deck and its proximity to the pond.

The problem was that the pine grove gave year-round shade, eliminating any solar heat gain, and the deck would have very little sun for nine months of the year. They loved that the living room would have a big view and the dining room would be nestled in the pine grove, but they were disappointed that the bedrooms were still not as quiet as they would like. They decided that the bridge was not a great idea after all because it would be difficult to get heavy household items, including groceries, into the house.

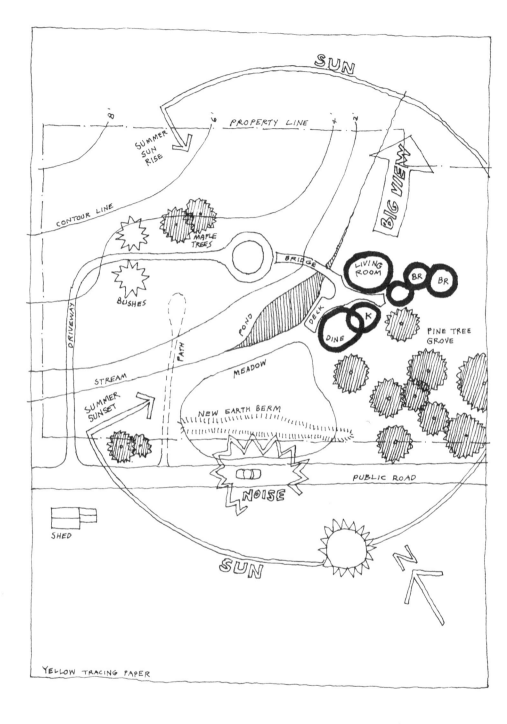

They decide again to keep diagramming. They are determined to have every room in an optimum location on their site.

Lois and Tom work until they feel they have considered most possibilities. Then they analyze all of their diagrams and choose the one that appears to fulfill most, if not all, of their requirements.

Shown here, the bubble arrangement represents a house that is as private as possible, that is away from the noise of the road, and has very quiet bedrooms. The living room has the big view and the dining room and kitchen enjoy access to a deck and intimate views of the pond and pine tree grove.

The bedrooms will get early morning sun and the dining room will get sunsets.

This location also makes use of the existing path as a walk to town directly from the entry. Lois also kept her romantic bridge over the stream as a way to get to the pine grove for picnics.

Tom and Lois are very happy. They feel that almost all of their goals have been reached, and they hadn't given up until they were successful. They are now ready to turn their bubble diagram into a three-dimensional design.

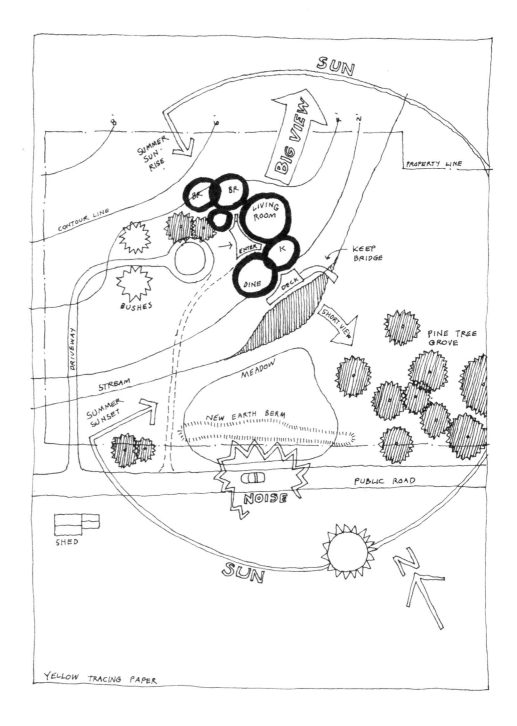

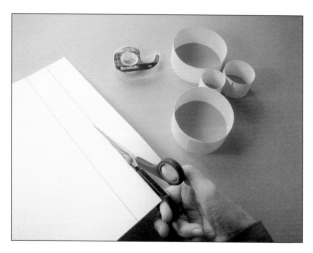

An interesting, simple transition step from designing with two-dimensional bubble drawings to starting a three-dimensional model is to build a tagboard bubble model of your design. This technique will help you visualize room relationships and begin to see how your building will relate to your site.

The drawing on the next page shows how Tom and Lois shaped their design with tagboard strips and some scotch tape.

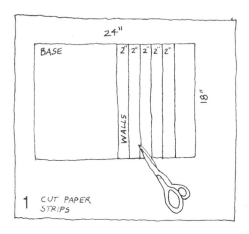

1 CUT PAPER STRIPS

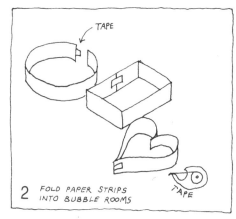

2 FOLD PAPER STRIPS INTO BUBBLE ROOMS

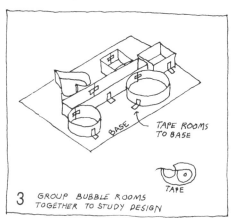

3 GROUP BUBBLE ROOMS TOGETHER TO STUDY DESIGN

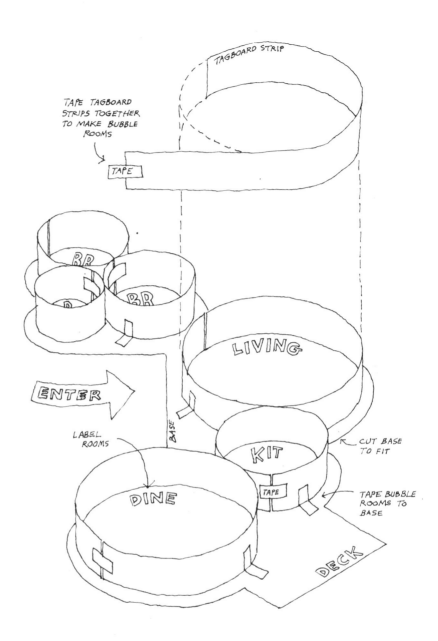

LEARNING KEY DESIGN PRINCIPLES

The last pages in this chapter will continue to demonstrate
how to turn your wish list and bubble diagram into a three-
dimensional design.

But first, let's take a break and consider a few key basic design
principles that concern the sun, ventilation, light, and space.

We want to always consider Mother Nature and how she will
react to our design. Also, we want to think about how *we* will feel
as we experience the inside of our new building.

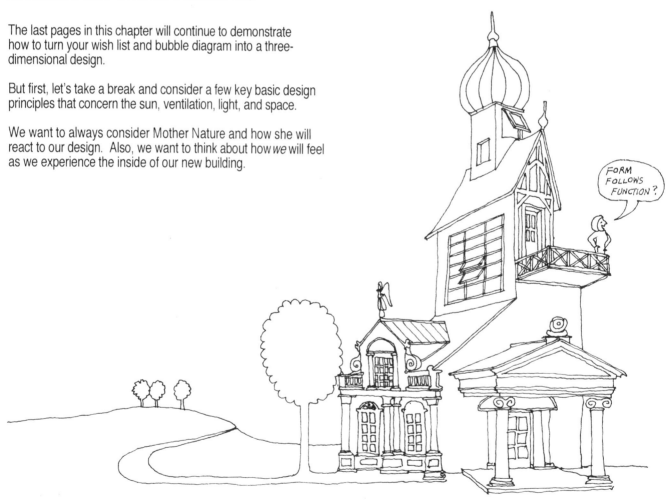

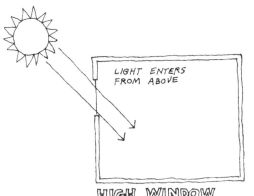
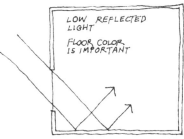

HIGH WINDOW

LIGHT ENTERS FROM ABOVE

LOW WINDOW

LOW REFLECTED LIGHT

FLOOR COLOR IS IMPORTANT

LIGHT

We often think of light as brightness that simply comes in a window. When we want more light, we design a bigger window. But there are many different ways that light can enter a space and change it for the better.

High windows can wash light over an entire room while low windows might brighten just the floor area. Deep windows or bay windows will create much reflected light – good to eliminate unwanted glare. Small windows can create a dramatic pin-hole of light and a large window can capture as much brightness or view as you desire. Light wells such as skylights or suntubes can make a windowless room full of light, and clerestory windows are an excellent method to bring north light into an artist's studio.

The colors of the walls, floor, and ceiling are very important, since most room light is reflected. Obviously, the lighter the colors, the brighter the room.

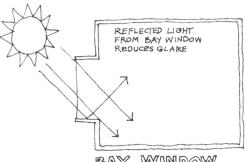

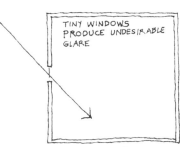

BAY WINDOW

REFLECTED LIGHT FROM BAY WINDOW REDUCES GLARE

SMALL WINDOW

TINY WINDOWS PRODUCE UNDESIRABLE GLARE

SKYLIGHT

SKYLIGHTS CAN BRING BRIGHT LIGHT INSIDE ROOMS.

CLERESTORY

FACING NORTH CAN BRING DESIRABLE NORTH LIGHT INTO A STUDIO

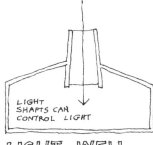
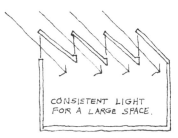

LIGHT WELL

LIGHT SHAFTS CAN CONTROL LIGHT

SAWTOOTH

CONSISTENT LIGHT FOR A LARGE SPACE.

SPACE

A home can be designed to include many different spaces, some light, some dark, high, low, rough, smooth, etc. Many spaces are purely personal, like a music room, some functional like a kitchen, and some poetic like a meditation room.

There are certain psychological responses to space which you can easily discover just by paying attention to how you feel when you are in an interesting space. A dark, cave-like space can inspire a quiet, protected, introverted feeling. The opposite would be a light, high, open space which might give you an extroverted, energetic feeling. These, of course, are simplified extremes, and there are many other possibilities. However, it is safe to say that the home that provides a wide variety of different spaces is one that will be more interesting, more reflective of your personality, and therefore more comfortable for you.

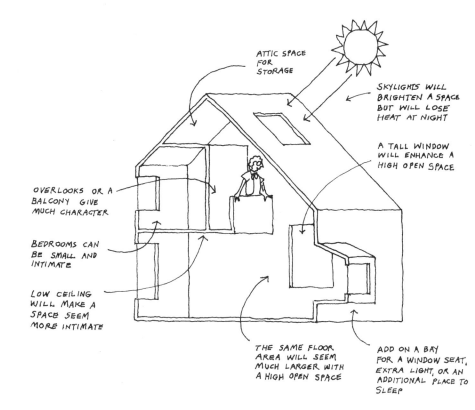

ATTIC SPACE
FOR
STORAGE

SKYLIGHTS WILL
BRIGHTEN A SPACE
BUT WILL LOSE
HEAT AT NIGHT

A TALL WINDOW
WILL ENHANCE A
HIGH OPEN SPACE

OVERLOOKS OR A
BALCONY GIVE
MUCH CHARACTER

BEDROOMS CAN
BE SMALL AND
INTIMATE

LOW CEILING
WILL MAKE A
SPACE SEEM
MORE INTIMATE

THE SAME FLOOR
AREA WILL SEEM
MUCH LARGER WITH
A HIGH OPEN SPACE

ADD ON A BAY
FOR A WINDOW SEAT,
EXTRA LIGHT, OR AN
ADDITIONAL PLACE TO
SLEEP

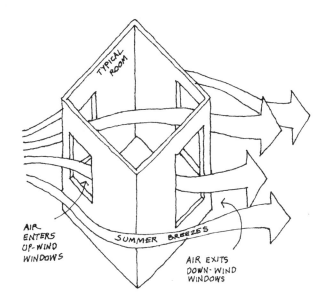

CROSS VENTILATION

VENTILATION

Everybody likes fresh air. In order to obtain it, good ventilation is a must for any home in any climate.

Natural ventilation will occur in a building when the up-wind and down-wind windows are open, allowing the flow of cooling breezes. We often call this *cross-ventilation*. Every major room in your house should be designed to give you the option of having good cross-ventilation.

When air heats up, it expands, causing it to become lighter and to rise inside a building. This is known as the *stack effect* and can be very useful in keeping your home cool in the hot summer months. By providing a high outlet in your design, you will naturally draw cooler air in through the lower inlets. High windows or skylights are commonly used for this purpose. A ceiling fan, known as a whole-house ventilator, can be used when this natural process needs to be amplified. The fan brings cool air into the house through the lower windows and expels the warm air through the attic.

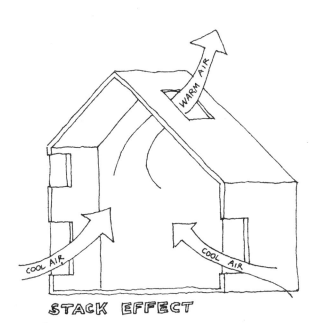

STACK EFFECT

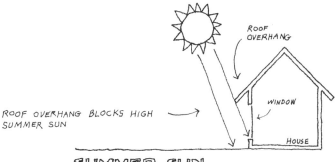

ROOF OVERHANG

ROOF OVERHANG BLOCKS HIGH →
SUMMER SUN

WINDOW

HOUSE

SUMMER SUN
OVERHANG

SOLAR HEAT

In cold climates, solar heat gain is obviously desirable and in warm climates, the opposite is true. A good house design will take advantage of the sun by absorbing its heat if the climate is cool and shading its rays if the climate is warm.

Roof overhangs and deciduous trees are excellent shading methods as they both allow winter sun to heat the house and both shade the sun's rays in the summer. Exterior shading such as this can cut 75% of the heat gain while interior shading (curtains) can cut only 20% of the heat gain.

In cool climates, all walls, floors, and roofs should be insulated. Windows should be triple-glazed. *Passive* solar heat can be collected with a dark-colored masonry mass (such as a floor) which will radiate heat over time. Solar collection devices such as photovoltaic cells are a developing technique used to heat entire buildings with the sun. The Internet is full of information on this subject.

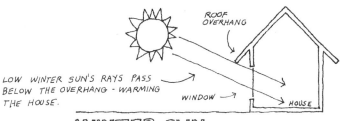

ROOF OVERHANG

LOW WINTER SUN'S RAYS PASS →
BELOW THE OVERHANG - WARMING
THE HOUSE.

WINDOW →

HOUSE

WINTER SUN
OVERHANG

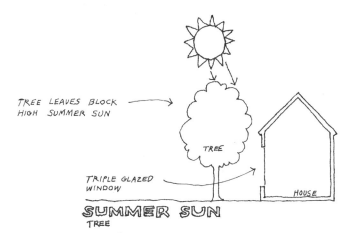

TREE LEAVES BLOCK →
HIGH SUMMER SUN

TREE

TRIPLE GLAZED
WINDOW

HOUSE

SUMMER SUN
TREE

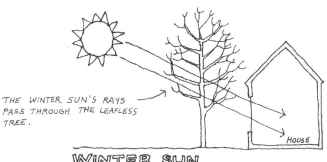

THE WINTER SUN'S RAYS
PASS THROUGH THE LEAFLESS
TREE.

HOUSE

WINTER SUN
TREE

MOVEMENT

A house is not a static piece of
sculpture, something to look
at. It is a grouping of spaces,
arranged to fit your needs.
As you move from one function
to another (for example, from
cooking to eating) you move
through one space into another.
Just as you feel differently being
in a unique space (for example,
a high, bright space or a low, dark
space), you will find that you also
feel differerent as you *move* from
one space to another.

As you pass from a high to a low
space you are most aware of the
difference at the moment you cross
between, and you'll find that each
space enhances the other. The
same is true from narrow to wide,
and from light to dark.

Be aware of these sensations and
include them in your design.

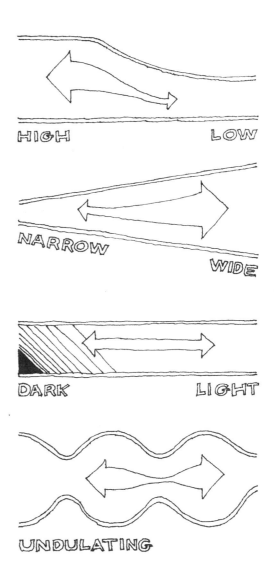

HIGH   LOW

NARROW   WIDE

DARK   LIGHT

UNDULATING

SHAPE

In the "Observing Houses" section in Chapter 4, it was shown that most homes are a collection of one or more basic solid geometric shapes. Even the most complicated house can be broken down into a grouping of these simple volumes.

Shown here are a few of the most popular house-building shapes.

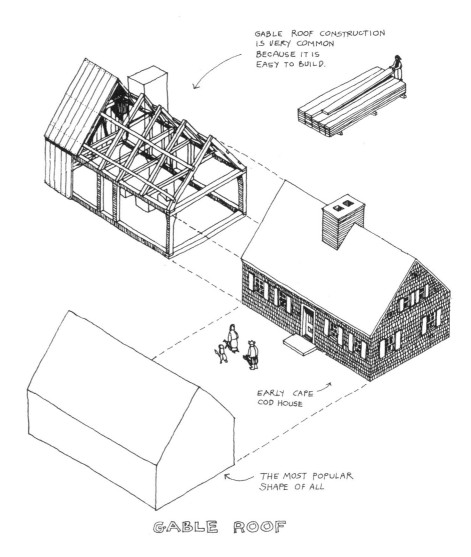

GABLE ROOF CONSTRUCTION IS VERY COMMON BECAUSE IT IS EASY TO BUILD.

EARLY CAPE COD HOUSE

THE MOST POPULAR SHAPE OF ALL

GABLE ROOF

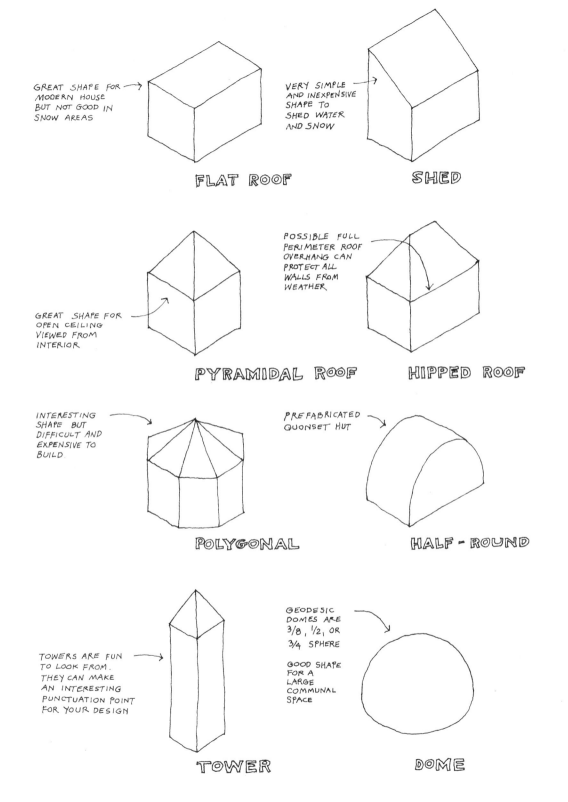

GREAT SHAPE FOR MODERN HOUSE BUT NOT GOOD IN SNOW AREAS

FLAT ROOF

VERY SIMPLE AND INEXPENSIVE SHAPE TO SHED WATER AND SNOW

SHED

GREAT SHAPE FOR OPEN CEILING VIEWED FROM INTERIOR

PYRAMIDAL ROOF

POSSIBLE FULL PERIMETER ROOF OVERHANG CAN PROTECT ALL WALLS FROM WEATHER

HIPPED ROOF

INTERESTING SHAPE BUT DIFFICULT AND EXPENSIVE TO BUILD.

POLYGONAL

PREFABRICATED QUONSET HUT

HALF - ROUND

TOWERS ARE FUN TO LOOK FROM. THEY CAN MAKE AN INTERESTING PUNCTUATION POINT FOR YOUR DESIGN

TOWER

GEODESIC DOMES ARE 3/8, 1/2, OR 3/4 SPHERE

GOOD SHAPE FOR A LARGE COMMUNAL SPACE

DOME

COMBINED SHAPES

By combining shapes, you will be able to manipulate your design to suit the uniqueness of your site and wish list program. There is an unlimited amount of configurations you can make with common shapes and an open mind.

Shown here are a few examples that may inspire you.

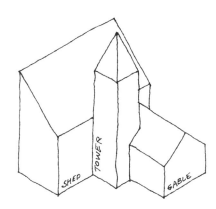

SHED DORMER FOR ADDITIONAL LIGHT

A SMALL GABLE AT RIGHT ANGLES TO THE ROOF CAN ACT AS A DORMER FOR ADDITIONAL LIGHT

GABLES
TRADITIONAL

SHEDS
CONTEMPORARY

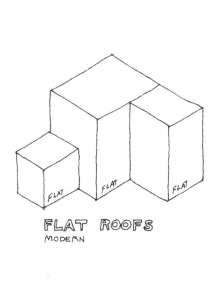

FLAT ROOFS
MODERN

SHED, GABLE, & TOWER
POST-MODERN

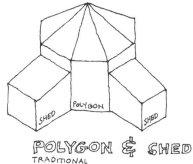

POLYGON & SHED
TRADITIONAL

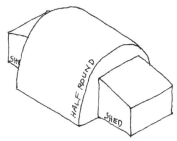

HALF-ROUND & SHED
FUNKY

Here is an old farmhouse that has received many additions over its long life. These shapes were added by necessity because of the addition of new family members and/or new farming and livestock needs. This is a good example of how buildings can grow because of an interior need or site consideration.

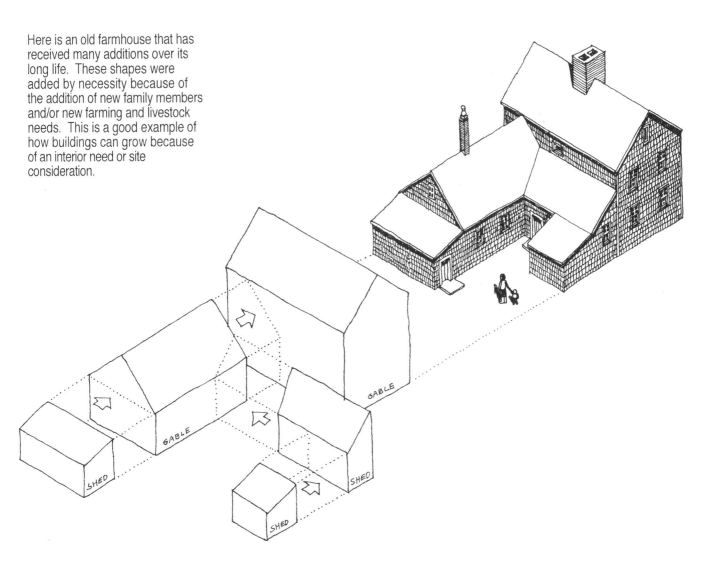

GABLE

GABLE

SHED

SHED

SHED

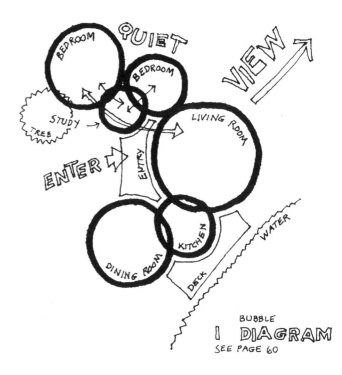

BUBBLE
1 DIAGRAM
SEE PAGE 60

DEFINING SHAPE

With the previous principles in mind, you are prepared to tackle the most exciting and important step of your work: the integration of all the information about your site and your wish list with your artistic visual images and dreams. It is this synthesis of function and aesthetics that makes architecture a unique art.

On these two pages is an illustration showing the home design process that begins with bubble diagrams and ends with a final shape for your house study model. This process will be detailed on the next few pages.

We'll be using Lois and Tom Sample's project as our example.

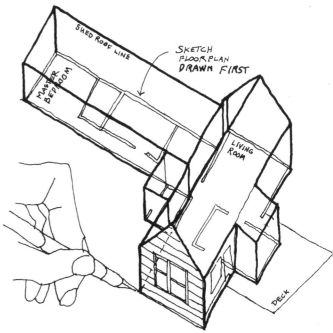

3 SKETCH SHAPES
OVER SKETCH FLOOR PLAN

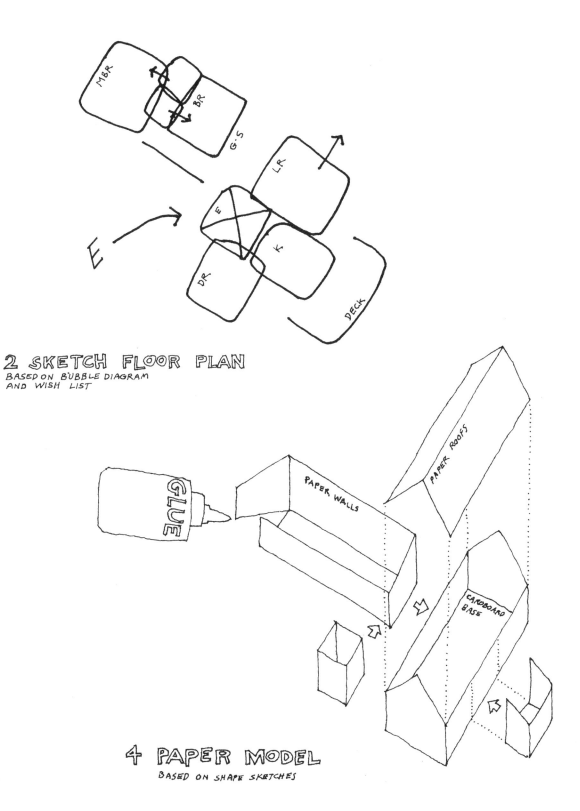

2 SKETCH FLOOR PLAN
BASED ON BUBBLE DIAGRAM
AND WISH LIST

4 PAPER MODEL
BASED ON SHAPE SKETCHES

81

SKETCHING YOUR PLAN

Once you've completed your bubble diagram and you're sure all the bubbles have found their proper places on your site, you're ready to start laying out your floor plan. Begin with simple lines, drawing freely at first, trying to create realistic "rooms" out of each bubble. Keep in mind that the bubble design is only a tool to help you organize the relationship of the spaces you plan for your house. Be flexible. If you find that you have a more interesting plan idea, don't hesitate to try it.

Shown here is Lois and Tom Sample's sketch evolution from bubble diagram into a working plan.

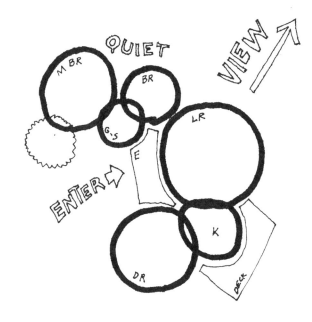

BUBBLE
DIAGRAM

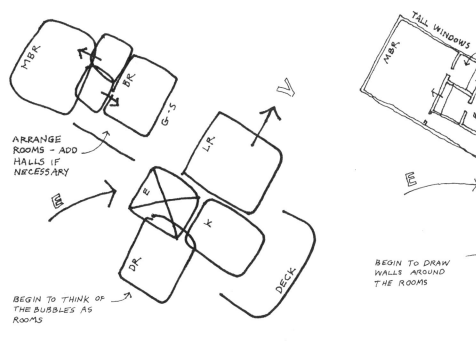

ARRANGE
ROOMS – ADD
HALLS IF
NECESSARY

BEGIN TO THINK OF
THE BUBBLES AS
ROOMS

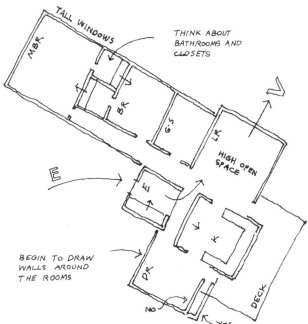

TALL WINDOWS

THINK ABOUT
BATHROOMS AND
CLOSETS

HIGH OPEN
SPACE

BEGIN TO DRAW
WALLS AROUND
THE ROOMS

NO

YES

2 SKETCH ROOMS

3 SKETCH WALLS

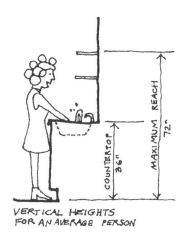

VERTICAL HEIGHTS
FOR AN AVERAGE PERSON

PLANNING YOUR KITCHEN

As you develop your sketch plan, you'll find that you need to know basic planning principles and typical dimensions for some of the more detailed parts of your work, such as the kitchen and the bathrooms.

The following two pages will give you some ideas to begin planning your kitchen. Simply put, if you think about the function of how your food progresses through your design, from storage (pantry or refrigerator) to washing, cooking, and serving, your kitchen will almost design itself. Equally important is the progression of dishware through your design, from storage (cupboards) to serving, washing (dishwasher), and back to storage. And don't forget your garbage disposal and recycling.

Keep these three primary functions (food flow, dishware flow, and garbage disposal) simple and your design will serve you well.

Here are a few kitchen plans showing cabinet and primary appliance layouts.

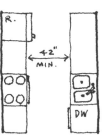

PARALLEL WALL

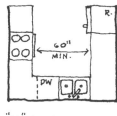

"U" SHAPE

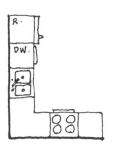

"L" SHAPE

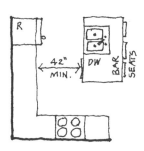

BROKEN "U" SHAPE

KITCHENETTE

Here is a kitchen plan that most kitchen experts would agree
is a very efficient, evolved design. Later, Tom and Lois will try to
adapt this design to their plan.

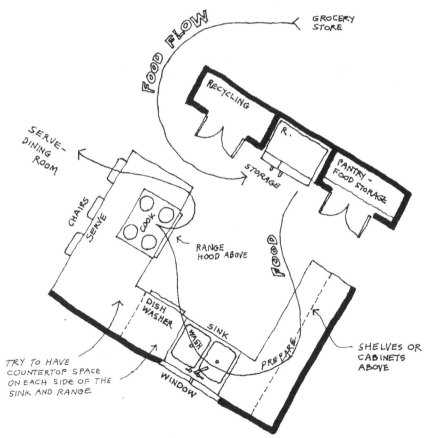

FOOD FLOW

GROCERY
STORE

RECYCLING

R.

STORAGE

PANTRY -
FOOD STORAGE

SERVE -
DINING
ROOM

CHAIRS

SERVE

COOK

RANGE
HOOD ABOVE

FOOD

DISH
WASHER

WASH

SINK

PREPARE

SHELVES OR
CABINETS
ABOVE

TRY TO HAVE
COUNTERTOP SPACE
ON EACH SIDE OF THE
SINK AND RANGE

WINDOW

PLANNING YOUR BATHROOMS

Here are some bathroom layouts showing the primary fixtures and their minimum clearance dimensions. If your budget is tight, it's a good idea to design a bath space that is minimal yet adequate. Bathrooms can be expensive.

TWO-FIXTURE BATHROOMS

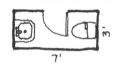

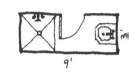

THREE-FIXTURE BATHROOMS

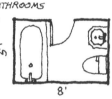
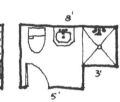

FOUR-FIXTURE BATHROOM

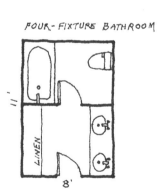

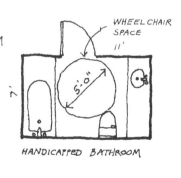

HANDICAPPED BATHROOM

VERTICAL HEIGHTS
FOR AN AVERAGE PERSON

Lois and Tom wanted to check their bathroom and kitchen cabinet design before they made their drawings. They built full-scale models from cardboard boxes to check their dimensions. A good idea.

Here is a popular bathroom sketch plan showing a four-fixture layout.

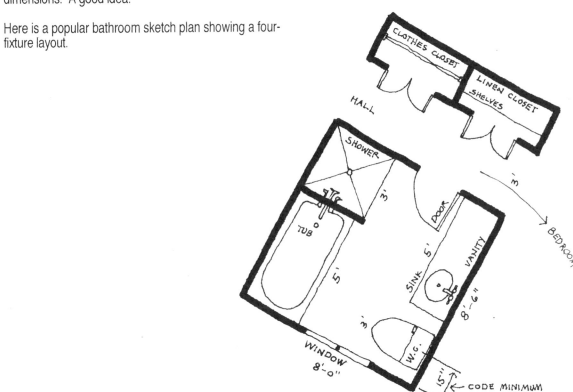

REVIEWING YOUR SKETCH PLAN

After you've reviewed and re-worked your study model,
you'll have to revisit your sketch plan and do the same to
it. This can best be illustrated by following Lois and Tom in
their attempt to make their house fit their needs and site as
perfectly as possible.

Since they cut the size of their bedroom wing and added a
second floor tower space over the entry, they have to make
changes to their plan so that it will conform to the changes
made with their model.

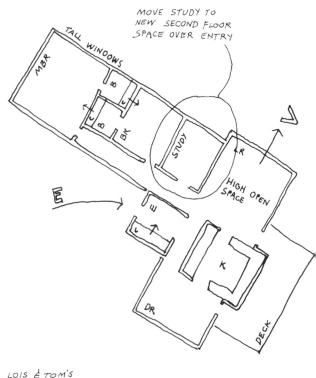

LOIS & TOM'S
FIRST SKETCH PLAN
FROM PAGE 83

Here is an illustration of the development of their new plan.
Note that they have also subtracted a full bathroom and
added a relocated half-bath to their plan.

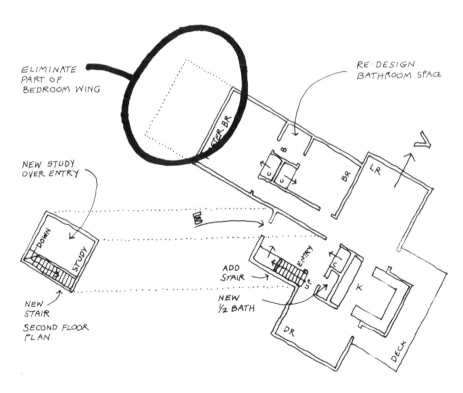

ELIMINATE
PART OF
BEDROOM WING

RE·DESIGN
BATHROOM SPACE

NEW STUDY
OVER ENTRY

MASTER BR.

B

C
C

BR

LR

DOWN

STUDY

ADD
STAIR

ENTRY

UP

K

NEW
STAIR

NEW
½ BATH

SECOND FLOOR
PLAN

DR

DECK

LOIS & TOM'S
REVISED SKETCH PLAN

STAIRS

Now that Lois and Tom have introduced a stair into their floor plan, it's time for a brief lesson on stair design.

Home designers have forever considered the stair as a focal point for their buildings. The early colonial homes placed the stair in the center of the design (center-hall plan) while the Victorians often located the stair in its own special space (stairwell). The detailing of the stair, the railings, ballusters, and treads, and the vertical circulation of its users, are all wonderful elements that can create a special detailed part of any building. Think about the stair in *Gone With the Wind* or the stair in Archie Bunker's house in *All In the Family.* Both are very special, character-giving places in their respective buildings.

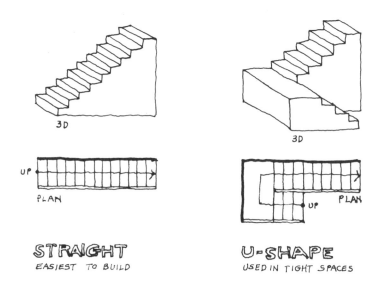

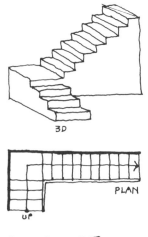

STRAIGHT
EASIEST TO BUILD

U-SHAPE
USED IN TIGHT SPACES

L-SHAPE
USED IN CORNERS

You must allow enough space in your design for an
adequate stair, and if you can, take advantage of it to make
your home interesting and exciting.

Here are some basic stair design principles and a few
dimensions to help you in designing your stair.

DETAILING YOUR SKETCH PLAN

Developing your sketch plan really means getting into more detail. Begin thinking about window and door locations, bathroom and kitchen layouts, closets, stairs, and other amenities such as fireplaces and wood-burning stoves. Use the symbols shown here to give more clarity and detail to your plan.

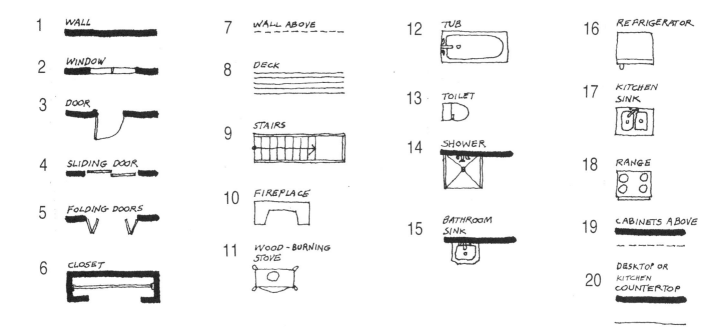

1 WALL

2 WINDOW

3 DOOR

4 SLIDING DOOR

5 FOLDING DOORS

6 CLOSET

7 WALL ABOVE

8 DECK

9 STAIRS

10 FIREPLACE

11 WOOD-BURNING STOVE

12 TUB

13 TOILET

14 SHOWER

15 BATHROOM SINK

16 REFRIGERATOR

17 KITCHEN SINK

18 RANGE

19 CABINETS ABOVE

20 DESKTOP OR KITCHEN COUNTERTOP

Here is a simple example of a house plan using all the symbols shown on the preceding page. We'll develop Lois and Tom Sample's plan on the next pages.

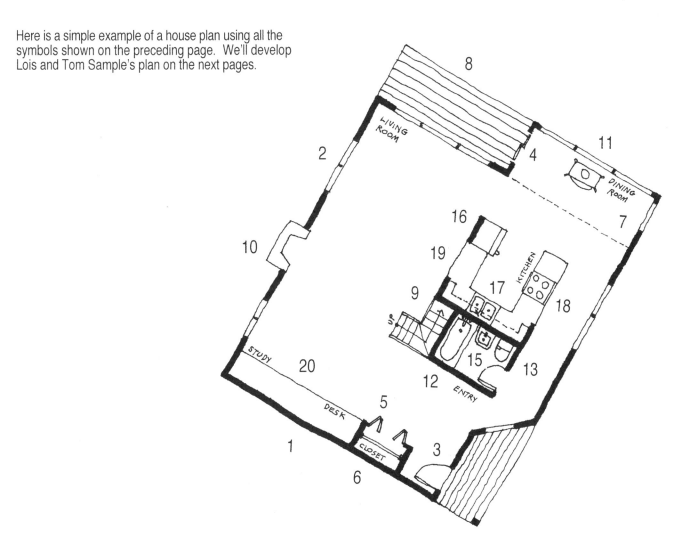

Lois and Tom worked hard to develop their sketch plan into a more detailed floor plan. The living room got a bit larger and gained a wood-burning stove. They added a master closet and a small deck off of their bedroom. They wanted both a tub and a shower in their bathroom, so they took the time to re-design these fixtures into the plan. More detail was added to the kitchen, and the front entry gained a bench/bookshelf unit.

Much to their delight, their design had become more personal, even though it was a very small house at 1430 square feet.

They re-read the chapter on scale on pages 30 and 31 and decided to make their drawing at the scale of 1/8"= 1'-0", or 1"= 8'. This is a common scale used by architects when designing houses.

Finally, Lois and Tom decided to draw their sketch plan in more detail using the collection of symbols shown on page 92 as a guide. Here is a full-size copy of their drawing.

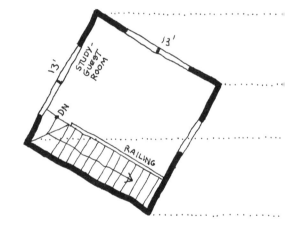

SECOND FLOOR PLAN
TOWER

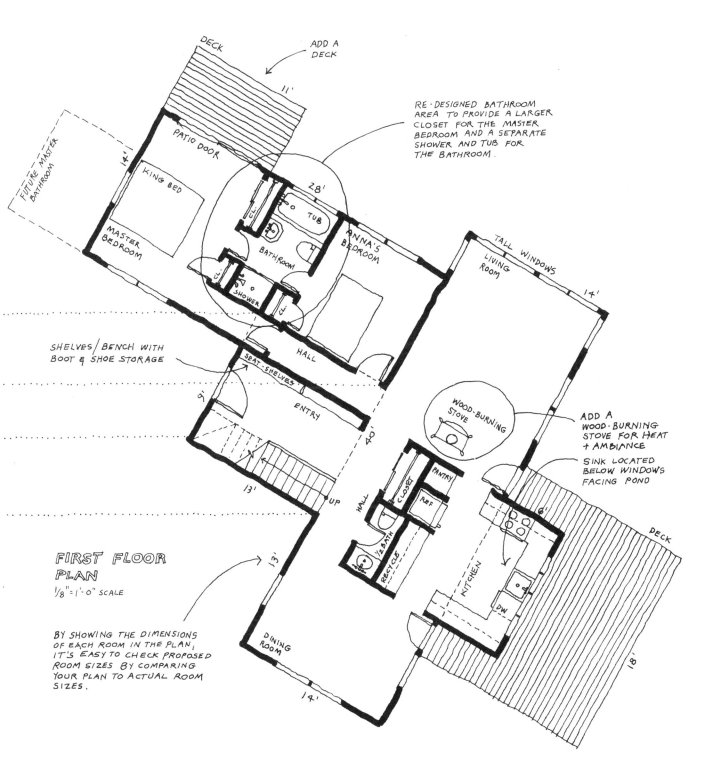

DECK

ADD A
DECK

11'

FUTURE MASTER BATHROOM

PATIO DOOR

14'

KING BED

MASTER BEDROOM

CL.

TUB

28'

BATHROOM

CL.

SHOWER

CL.

ANNA'S BEDROOM

RE-DESIGNED BATHROOM AREA TO PROVIDE A LARGER CLOSET FOR THE MASTER BEDROOM AND A SEPARATE SHOWER AND TUB FOR THE BATHROOM.

TALL WINDOWS

LIVING ROOM

14'

SHELVES/BENCH WITH BOOT & SHOE STORAGE

HALL

SEAT·SHELVES·

9'

ENTRY

40'

WOOD-BURNING STOVE

ADD A WOOD-BURNING STOVE FOR HEAT + AMBIANCE

13'

UP

HALL

CLOSET

PANTRY

REF.

1/2 BATH

RECYCLE

KITCHEN

6'

SINK LOCATED BELOW WINDOWS FACING POND

DECK

DW

FIRST FLOOR PLAN
1/8"=1'-0" SCALE

13'

DINING ROOM

BY SHOWING THE DIMENSIONS OF EACH ROOM IN THE PLAN, IT'S EASY TO CHECK PROPOSED ROOM SIZES BY COMPARING YOUR PLAN TO ACTUAL ROOM SIZES.

14'

18'

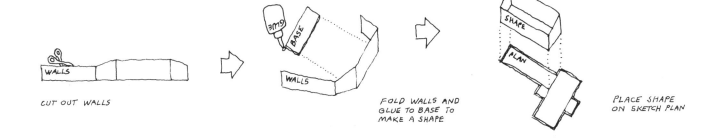

CUT OUT WALLS   FOLD WALLS AND GLUE TO BASE TO MAKE A SHAPE   PLACE SHAPE ON SKETCH PLAN

LOIS AND TOM BUILD A STUDY MODEL

Lois and Tom continue to work. They decide that it's time to build a study model to get an idea how their sketch plan will look in three dimensions.

They start by laying out the walls of the various parts of the house. Then they fold the walls to make a four-sided model. Next, they glue a cardboard base to the bottom of each shape and add a folded paper roof piece to the top. Shown below are the ribbon-like walls of the four major parts of Lois and Tom's house.

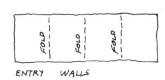

ENTRY WALLS

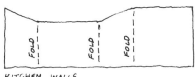

KITCHEN WALLS

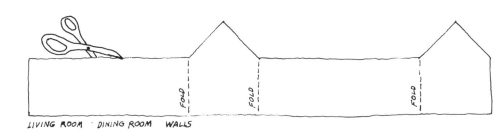

LIVING ROOM · DINING ROOM WALLS

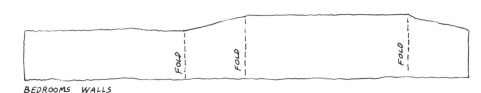

BEDROOMS WALLS

1 CUT OUT WALLS

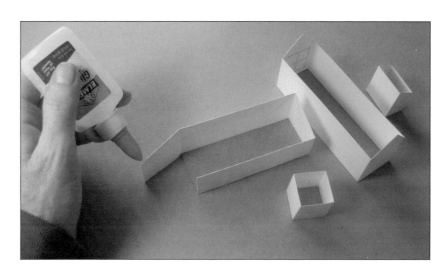

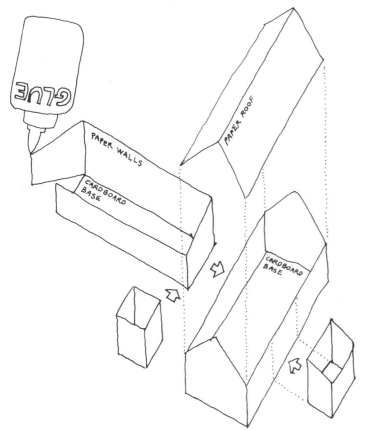

2 GLUE WALLS TO BASE

Labels within the illustration: GLUE, PAPER WALLS, PAPER ROOF, CARDBOARD BASE, CARDBOARD BASE

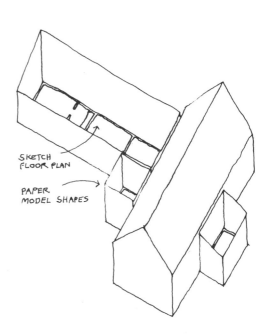

3 PLACE SHAPES OVER PLAN

Labels within the illustration: SKETCH FLOOR PLAN, PAPER MODEL SHAPES

Lois and Tom are disappointed to find that their study model reveals their design to be too conventional and a bit sprawling. They decide to reduce the size of the bedroom wing by relocating the study in a new tower over the entry. Wow! What a great idea! This new second floor room is now a very special space with wonderful light, air, and views. And, the entry becomes much more interesting because you are now entering a tower.

The house has changed from a banal one-story building to a more interesting grouping of shapes with a new stair and a small second floor. Better yet, it has a nice sculptural quality and seems more inviting. Only their study model could have led Lois and Tom to this new exciting design. They are happy they took the time to build and plan with it.

SUBTRACT PART OF
BEDROOM WING

BEDROOM WING

ENTER

PAPER MODEL

ADD NEW
TOWER WITH
ENTRY ON THE
GROUND FLOOR
AND STUDY
ABOVE

PYRAMIDAL ROOF
ON NEW TOWER

ENTER

MODEL

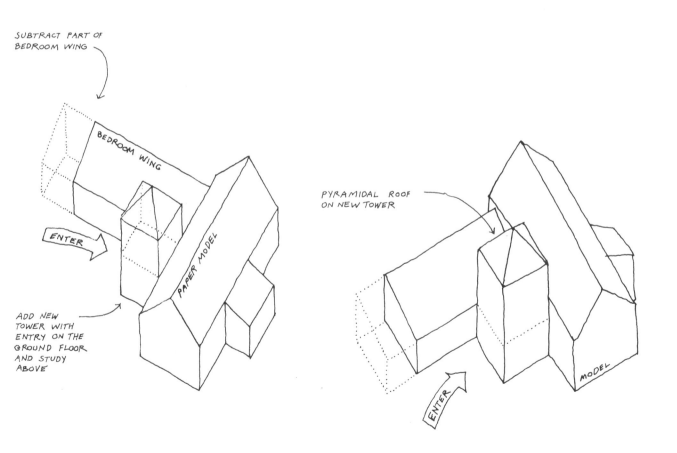

DESIGNING YOUR WINDOWS

The thoughtful placement of windows in your rooms is the single most important task yet to be completed. It will create the interior ambiance you desire. Windows are used primarily for daytime light, to frame an outside view, or to allow in fresh air. The amount of light, view, or air you want in each room needs to be carefully considered. For example, you may want floods of direct sunlight in the living room or kitchen and very little indirect (north) light in your bedrooms. You may want your dining room to have a view of your garden and your living room to have a view of the distant horizon and sky. Try to imagine yourself in each room, looking out.

It's best to design window size and location first from the inside of your house, allowing them to be dependent on the needs of each room. After you've done this, don't worry if the outside of your house looks a bit crazy. Just try to simplify the window design from the outside while keeping your inside window requirements for light, view, and air the same. This will require some studying – designing from the inside, then from the outside, going back and forth until you reach a compromise design that you like.

Your model can be quite a useful tool in helping to design your windows. The easiest approach is to carefully draw the windows on each facade of your model.

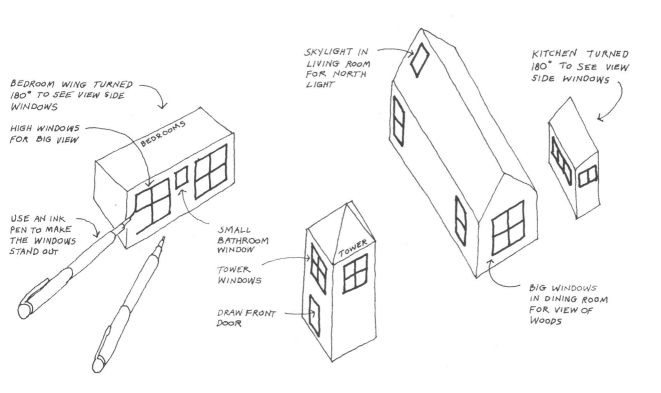

BEDROOM WING TURNED
180° TO SEE VIEW SIDE
WINDOWS

HIGH WINDOWS
FOR BIG VIEW

USE AN INK
PEN TO MAKE
THE WINDOWS
STAND OUT

BEDROOMS

SMALL
BATHROOM
WINDOW

TOWER
WINDOWS

DRAW FRONT
DOOR

TOWER

SKYLIGHT IN
LIVING ROOM
FOR NORTH
LIGHT

KITCHEN TURNED
180° TO SEE VIEW
SIDE WINDOWS

BIG WINDOWS
IN DINING ROOM
FOR VIEW OF
WOODS

A better approach to studying your window design is to cut out the windows before you finally assemble your model. This method is more time-consuming but is often worth it because you can take your model to your site and actually see how the light enters the windows by holding it up to the sun.

Shown here are some instructions on how to cut out your windows on your model.

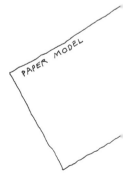

SMOOTH "SHIRT BACK" CARDBOARD ACTS AS A GOOD CUTTING BASE

PAPER MODEL

DANGER

I'VE GOT THE BANDAIDS!

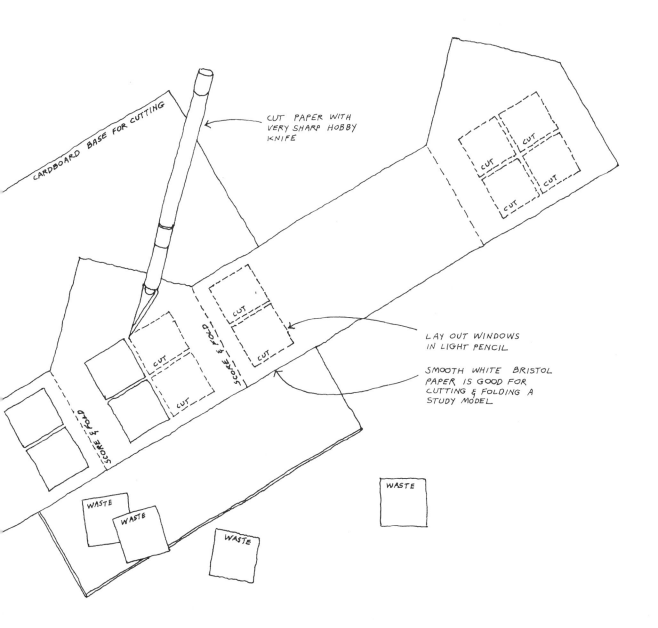

CARDBOARD BASE FOR CUTTING

CUT PAPER WITH
VERY SHARP HOBBY
KNIFE

CUT

CUT

CUT

CUT

SCORE & FOLD

CUT

CUT

SCORE & FOLD

CUT

CUT

LAY OUT WINDOWS
IN LIGHT PENCIL

SMOOTH WHITE BRISTOL
PAPER IS GOOD FOR
CUTTING & FOLDING A
STUDY MODEL

WASTE

WASTE

WASTE

WASTE

LOIS AND TOM FINISH THEIR DESIGN

Lois and Tom felt that the cut-out windows were the most
helpful for their understanding of their design. They decided
to rebuild their model with cut-out windows. They re-cut the
walls and then cut out the windows before glueing their
model together.

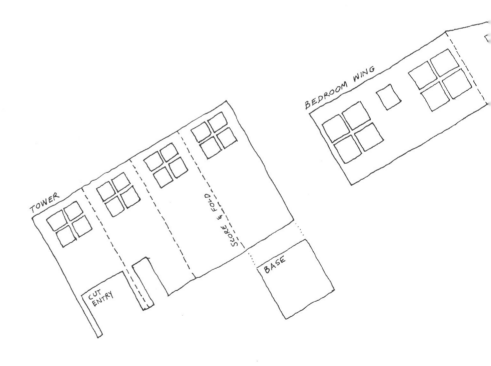

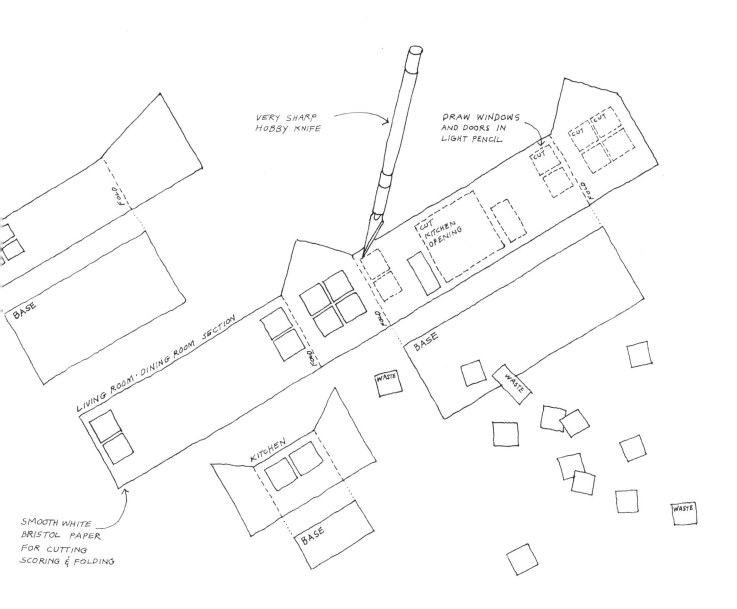

VERY SHARP
HOBBY KNIFE

DRAW WINDOWS
AND DOORS IN
LIGHT PENCIL

FOLD

BASE

CUT

CUT

CUT

FOLD

CUT
KITCHEN
OPENING

FOLD

BASE

LIVING ROOM · DINING ROOM SECTION

FOLD

WASTE

WASTE

KITCHEN

BASE

SMOOTH WHITE
BRISTOL PAPER
FOR CUTTING
SCORING & FOLDING

WASTE

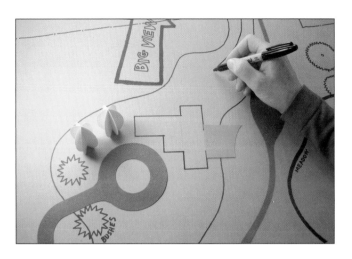

Folding and glueing model

Lois and Tom decided to sketch their site plan at the same scale as their house model, on a large sheet of paper, to see how their design fits with the various constraints of their lot. This is a good way to see how your house will react to the nature of your site.

They installed two paper trees, the deck, and the driveway so they could fully appreciate their design. They love their house because it really suits their needs and their site, and they are thrilled because they designed it themselves.

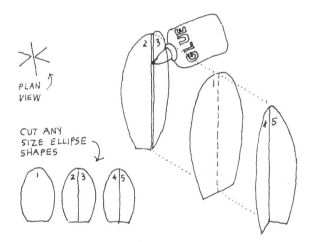

PLAN
VIEW

CUT ANY
SIZE ELLIPSE
SHAPES

HOW TO MAKE A PAPER TREE

Model on sketch site plan, viewed from the east

Model on sketch site plan, viewed from the south

Use most of your windows for viewside light to bring the outdoors in and to make your space feel larger than it is.

6 SPECIFYING YOUR HOUSE PARTS

The four most important elements of your house aesthetic that you will want to understand and design are windows, doors, roofing, and siding. These elements play key roles in the style or "look" of your new home.

Visit building supply stores, like Lowe's and Home Depot, and specialty window and door stores to actually see the products you like. Get catalogs of these materials and read them. Set up a file for each of the four categories, as discussed on page 26, and fill them with photos, flyer information gleaned from the catalogs, and your own notes. These files will be helpful when it comes time to make your choices.

The two most important elements of your house involving its efficiency, or comfort, are insulation and heating/cooling. These elements can be researched by using the Internet, but a second helpful method is to have a meeting with a local insulation installer and a heating/cooling engineer. These tradesmen are more than willing to visit with you to discuss your new home. They will tell you what is required and what is best for you within a range of choices. They will also be happy to do the work once you've decided on the type of insulation and heating system you'll use.

The next few pages will give you a quick introduction to these six major elements and then show you how to indicate them on sketch drawings of the exterior of your house design.

CHOOSING YOUR WINDOW TYPES

After you have decided the location and size of your windows, you'll need to know all about the various types of windows that are commercially available. There are three basic types: sliding, swinging, and fixed. Each of these comes in a wide variety of sizes and shapes. They can be single glazed for temperate climates and double, or even triple, glazed for better insulation in very extreme climates.

A visit to a window sales room will help to educate you about all the window types available. Most salespeople are very happy to discuss the windows in each of the rooms of your home. Your model will be a big help in illustrating your ideas.

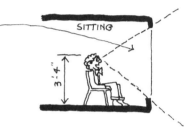

PICTURE WINDOW GOOD FOR FULL VIEW

SITTING

3'-4"

TRY TO AVOID HORIZONTAL WINDOW DIVISIONS AT CRITICAL EYE LEVEL HEIGHTS

DINING

EYES

2'-8"

4'-0"

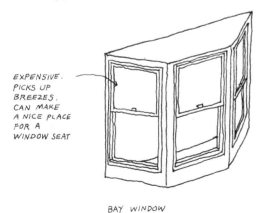

EXPENSIVE. PICKS UP BREEZES. CAN MAKE A NICE PLACE FOR A WINDOW SEAT

BAY WINDOW

COOKING

EYES

5'-2"

3'-6"

LEAVE ENOUGH WALL SPACE (AT LEAST 3'-6") FOR KITCHEN CABINETS

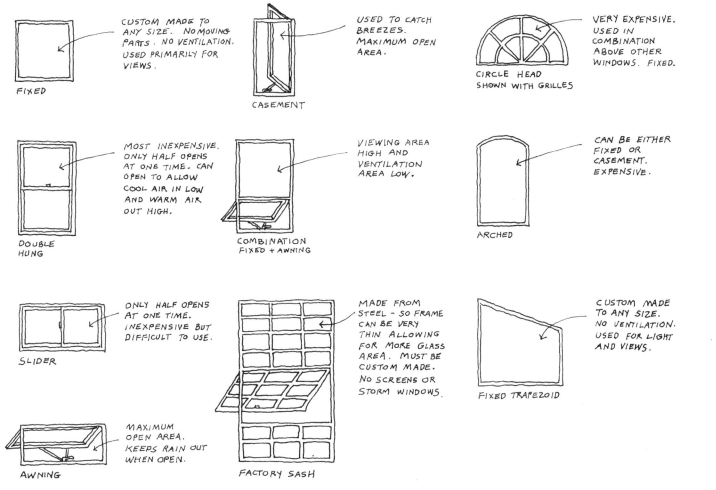

FIXED — CUSTOM MADE TO ANY SIZE. NO MOVING PARTS. NO VENTILATION. USED PRIMARILY FOR VIEWS.

CASEMENT — USED TO CATCH BREEZES. MAXIMUM OPEN AREA.

CIRCLE HEAD SHOWN WITH GRILLES — VERY EXPENSIVE. USED IN COMBINATION ABOVE OTHER WINDOWS. FIXED.

DOUBLE HUNG — MOST INEXPENSIVE. ONLY HALF OPENS AT ONE TIME. CAN OPEN TO ALLOW COOL AIR IN LOW AND WARM AIR OUT HIGH.

COMBINATION FIXED + AWNING — VIEWING AREA HIGH AND VENTILATION AREA LOW.

ARCHED — CAN BE EITHER FIXED OR CASEMENT. EXPENSIVE.

SLIDER — ONLY HALF OPENS AT ONE TIME. INEXPENSIVE BUT DIFFICULT TO USE.

FACTORY SASH — MADE FROM STEEL – SO FRAME CAN BE VERY THIN ALLOWING FOR MORE GLASS AREA. MUST BE CUSTOM MADE. NO SCREENS OR STORM WINDOWS.

FIXED TRAPEZOID — CUSTOM MADE TO ANY SIZE. NO VENTILATION. USED FOR LIGHT AND VIEWS.

AWNING — MAXIMUM OPEN AREA. KEEPS RAIN OUT WHEN OPEN.

CHOOSING YOUR DOORS

Doors are the key moving part of your design. They are in constant use, providing privacy, light, fresh air, and sound control to every room in your home. Each door must be given careful consideration to allow for the smooth functioning of your home.

Most doors are 6'-8" high by various widths, from bathroom doors, starting at 2'-0" wide, to bedroom doors, usually 2'-6 wide, to your front door, which is usually 3'-0" wide. Doors are usually manufactured and brought to the buillding site pre-hinged and in their frame. This makes installation easy.

Sliding glass doors are a good way to allow lots of light and air into a room while still offering use as a door.

Your building supply store will have examples of both interior and exterior doors for you to test. Get the specifications of your favorites and put them in your files. You'll be locating them on your floor-plan drawing later.

NOW THIS IS A NICE DOOR!

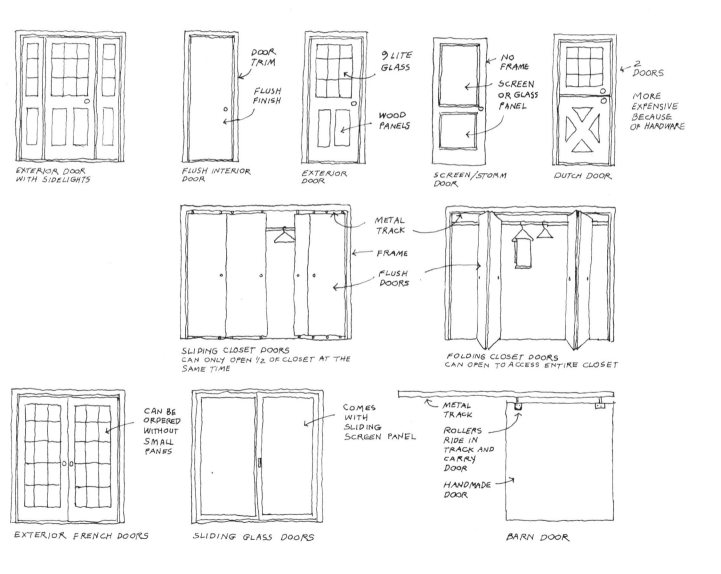

EXTERIOR DOOR
WITH SIDELIGHTS

FLUSH INTERIOR
DOOR

DOOR
TRIM

FLUSH
FINISH

EXTERIOR
DOOR

9 LITE
GLASS

WOOD
PANELS

SCREEN/STORM
DOOR

NO
FRAME

SCREEN
OR GLASS
PANEL

DUTCH DOOR

2 DOORS

MORE
EXPENSIVE
BECAUSE
OF HARDWARE

SLIDING CLOSET DOORS
CAN ONLY OPEN 1/2 OF CLOSET AT THE
SAME TIME

METAL
TRACK

FRAME

FLUSH
DOORS

FOLDING CLOSET DOORS
CAN OPEN TO ACCESS ENTIRE CLOSET

EXTERIOR FRENCH DOORS

CAN BE
ORDERED
WITHOUT
SMALL
PANES

SLIDING GLASS DOORS

COMES
WITH
SLIDING
SCREEN PANEL

BARN DOOR

METAL
TRACK

ROLLERS
RIDE IN
TRACK AND
CARRY
DOOR

HANDMADE
DOOR

CHOOSING YOUR SIDING

Exterior siding is the finish material that is attached to the sides of your house to weatherproof the walls. This choice is important since it is the major exterior surface of your home and will set the tone for your outside aesthetic.

Usually, all of the exterior walls of a framed house are covered with a layer of 1/2" construction-grade plywood – commonly called sheathing. This sheathing adds great strength to the structure and provides a nailing surface for the finish material. A layer of tar paper or house-wrap material is usually stapled over the sheathing for extra weather protection before the finish siding is installed.

Your building supply store or local lumberyard will display most popular siding materials. A brief visit there will be a good hands-on start in educating yourself as to what is available and what siding material is best for you.

Next, start looking at the siding materials of buildings as you travel around your neighborhood. You'll see clapboards on colonial homes, novelty siding on bungalows, board and batten on out-buildings, wood shingles on vacation houses, vinyl siding on split levels, and plywood siding on inexpensive construction. Decide what you like, take a photo or two, and file your choice.

Here is a quick lesson of the most popular siding materials available today.

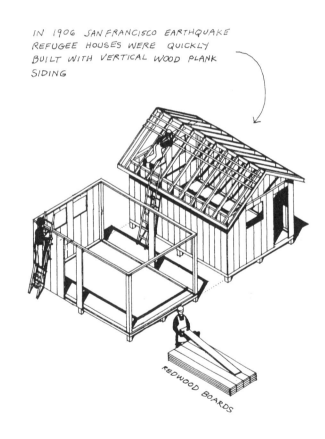

IN 1906 SAN FRANCISCO EARTHQUAKE REFUGEE HOUSES WERE QUICKLY BUILT WITH VERTICAL WOOD PLANK SIDING

REDWOOD BOARDS

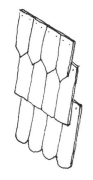
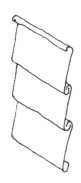
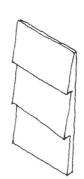
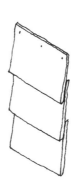
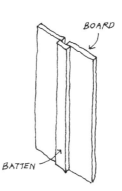

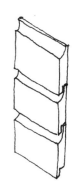

BOARD

BATTEN

WOOD SHINGLES
DURABLE
BEAUTIFUL
EXPENSIVE LABOR

ALUMINUM OR
VINYL
NO MAINTENANCE
VERY DURABLE

FIBER-CEMENT
BOARD
NO MAINTENANCE
INSTALLED PAINTED

WOOD
CLAPBOARDS
TRADITIONAL
NATURAL WOOD
OR PAINT

WOOD BOARD
AND BATTEN
INEXPENSIVE
DEEP VERTICAL
LINES

VERTICAL WOOD
TONGUE AND
GROOVE
FLUSH BOARDS
INEXPENSIVE

NOVELTY
WOOD
INEXPENSIVE
DEEP HORIZONTAL
LINES

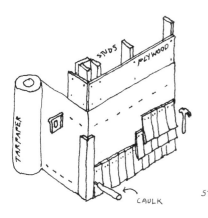
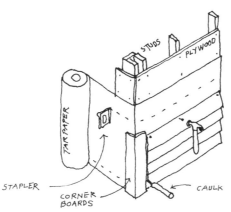
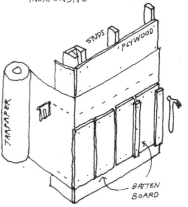

STUDS   PLYWOOD
TARPAPER
CAULK

INSTALLING WOOD SHINGLES
LABOR INTENSIVE

STUDS   PLYWOOD
TARPAPER
STAPLER
CORNER
BOARDS
CAULK

INSTALLING WOOD CLAPBOARDS
CEDAR NEEDS CARE BUT
IS BEAUTIFUL
TAKES PAINT WELL

STUDS   PLYWOOD
TARPAPER
BATTEN
BOARD

INSTALLING BOARD AND BATTEN
SIDING
LOOKS GREAT PAINTED
INEXPENSIVE

115

CHOOSING YOUR ROOF

Roofing is one of the primary visible exterior surfaces of your home, so you must take care as you make your selection. Color, texture, longevity, and of course, cost must all be considered.

The Internet can get you started and will be excellent in helping you narrow down your roofing decision, but before you make your final choice, you should consult with a roofing installer. He will tell you that any shaped roof is possible, even flat. He can inform you about cost, color, and texture, and can provide you with samples and methods of construction which may affect your decision.

Your building supply store will display most popular roofing materials and can also provide answers to many of your questions.

Here is a brief lesson to familiarize you with some roofing possibilities.

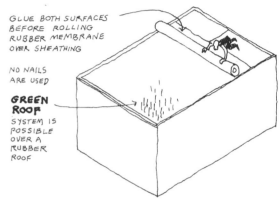

GLUE BOTH SURFACES BEFORE ROLLING RUBBER MEMBRANE OVER SHEATHING

NO NAILS ARE USED

GREEN ROOF SYSTEM IS POSSIBLE OVER A RUBBER ROOF

EPDM (ETHYLENE PROPYLENE DIENE MONOMER) OR RUBBER ROOFING BEST FOR FLAT ROOFS

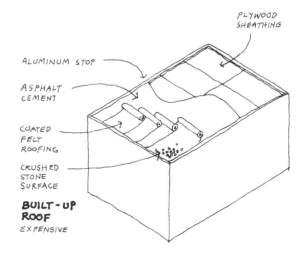

PLYWOOD SHEATHING

ALUMINUM STOP

ASPHALT CEMENT

COATED FELT ROOFING

CRUSHED STONE SURFACE

BUILT-UP ROOF EXPENSIVE

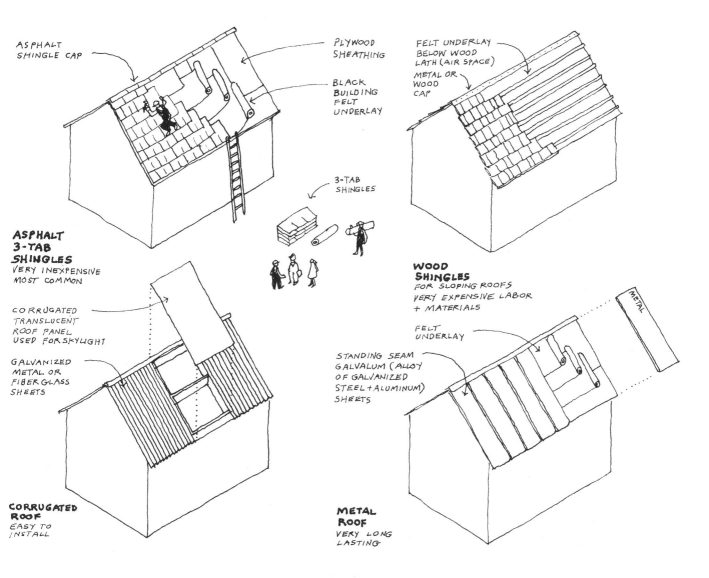

ASPHALT
SHINGLE CAP

PLYWOOD
SHEATHING

BLACK
BUILDING
FELT
UNDERLAY

**ASPHALT
3-TAB
SHINGLES**
VERY INEXPENSIVE
MOST COMMON

3-TAB
SHINGLES

FELT UNDERLAY
BELOW WOOD
LATH (AIR SPACE)

METAL OR
WOOD
CAP

**WOOD
SHINGLES**
FOR SLOPING ROOFS
VERY EXPENSIVE LABOR
+ MATERIALS

CORRUGATED
TRANSLUCENT
ROOF PANEL
USED FOR SKYLIGHT

GALVANIZED
METAL OR
FIBERGLASS
SHEETS

**CORRUGATED
ROOF**
EASY TO
INSTALL

FELT
UNDERLAY

STANDING SEAM
GALVALUM (ALLOY
OF GALVANIZED
STEEL + ALUMINUM)
SHEETS

METAL

**METAL
ROOF**
VERY LONG
LASTING

CHOOSING YOUR INSULATION

Insulation is the blanket of material that surrounds your house to retain heat or cool air. There are many different types of insulation, all having a rating that tells you the ability of the material to resist the flow of heat. This rating is called an R-value. A brief visit to your local building inspector or mechanical engineer will inform you as to what R-value is required or desired in your walls, floors, and ceilings. Also, a visit to your local building supply store can give you a hands-on education.

Typical required R-values for ceilings range from 15 to 50, for walls from 10 to 25 and for floors from 10 to 30, depending on your climate. A good mechanical engineer or an insulation installer, who carries all types of insulation material, will be able to help you choose the best type of insulation for all the surfaces of your home.

Insulation is a relatively inexpensive part of your home. Don't hesitate to over-insulate. Payback from your heating bills will start immediately.

Here is a quick lesson to inform you of the wide variety of popular insulation materials.

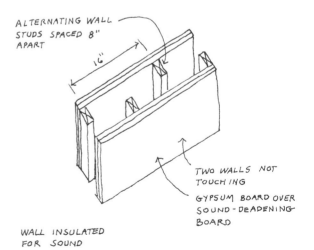

ALTERNATING WALL STUDS SPACED 8" APART

16"

TWO WALLS NOT TOUCHING

GYPSUM BOARD OVER SOUND-DEADENING BOARD

WALL INSULATED FOR SOUND

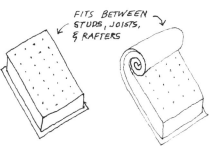

BLANKET
MINERAL FIBROUS
GLASS OR ROCK
SPUN INTO THIN
FIBERS · FIBERGLASS

FITS BETWEEN
STUDS, JOISTS,
& RAFTERS

BATT
MINERAL FIBROUS
GLASS OR ROCK
SPUN INTO THIN
FIBERS · FIBERGLASS

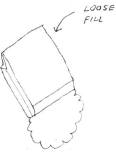

LOOSE
FILL

MINERAL CELLULAR
VERMICULITE,
PERLITE OR FOAMED
GLASS

RIGID

ORGANIC CELLULAR
POLYSTYRENE
POLYURETHANE
CORK

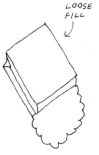

LOOSE
FILL

ORGANIC FIBROUS
COTTON, HAIR
CELLULOSE

FOAM
EXPANDS

HOSE

SPRAY

**SPRAYED
ORGANIC CELLULAR**
ISONINE
POLYURETHANE

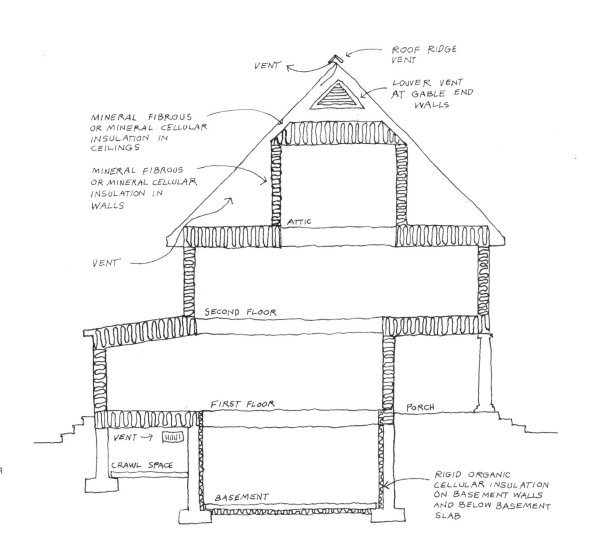

ROOF RIDGE
VENT

VENT

LOUVER VENT
AT GABLE END
WALLS

MINERAL FIBROUS
OR MINERAL CELLULAR
INSULATION IN
CEILINGS

MINERAL FIBROUS
OR MINERAL CELLULAR
INSULATION IN
WALLS

ATTIC

VENT

SECOND FLOOR

FIRST FLOOR

PORCH

VENT →

CRAWL SPACE

BASEMENT

RIGID ORGANIC
CELLULAR INSULATION
ON BASEMENT WALLS
AND BELOW BASEMENT
SLAB

INSULATING FOR A
COLD CLIMATE
CUT-AWAY VIEW OF
INSULATED HOUSE

CHOOSING YOUR HEATING/COOLING SYSTEM

There are many different heating and cooling systems that can be installed in your home. Careful planning with a mechanical engineer or a well-reputed heating/air-conditioning company is necessary.

The most expensive systems, such as geothermal and solar, will provide the lowest fuel bills. The least expensive to install, electric, is the most expensive to operate. And the most popular systems, forced air and baseboard/radiant hot water, use fossil fuels.

All heating and cooling systems have their pros and cons. It's best to meet with local experts, learn what is available, consider your climate and your budget, then choose what is best for you.

Here is a brief introduction to the most popular heating/cooling systems that you may want to consider.

WOOD-BURNING STOVES ARE THE LEAST EXPENSIVE HEATING SYSTEMS TO INSTALL AND OPERATE

FORCED AIR

NOISY

SPACE CONSUMING DUCTS

ACCOMMODATES HEATING AND COOLING SYSTEMS

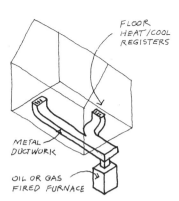

FLOOR HEAT/COOL REGISTERS

METAL DUCTWORK

OIL OR GAS FIRED FURNACE

ELECTRIC BASEBOARD

INEXPENSIVE TO INSTALL

VERY EXPENSIVE TO OPERATE

DRY HEAT

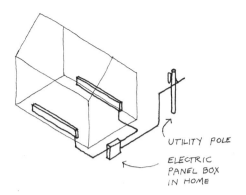

UTILITY POLE

ELECTRIC PANEL BOX IN HOME

SOLAR

EXPENSIVE TO INSTALL

LOW OPERATION COST

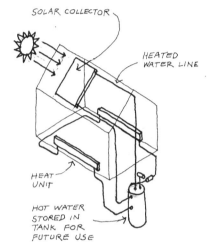

SOLAR COLLECTOR

HEATED WATER LINE

HEAT UNIT

HOT WATER STORED IN TANK FOR FUTURE USE

GEO THERMAL

EXPENSIVE TO INSTALL

VERY LOW OPERATION COST

WARM FLOORS

HOT OR COLD WATER TUBES ARE INSTALLED BELOW THE FINISHED FLOOR

GEOTHERMAL HEAT PUMP UNIT

WATER PIPE LOOPS IN DRILLED WELLS ABSORB HEAT OR COLD FROM GROUND AND TRANSFER IT TO YOUR HOME

HOT-WATER BASEBOARD

VERY COMFORTABLE

EASY TO MAINTAIN

USES FOSSIL FUELS

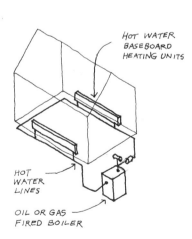

HOT WATER BASEBOARD HEATING UNITS

HOT WATER LINES

OIL OR GAS FIRED BOILER

Don't be afraid to use flat roofs: roof technology has greatly improved and the modern look that flat roofs afford is rapidly gaining favor.

7 COMPLETING YOUR DRAWINGS

You will use your drawings to convey most of the important decisions made during the design process. Simply put, they are sketches of the exterior of your house, as described in Chapter 4, illustrating its shape, its plan, some of its important dimensions, and the materials you plan to use.

Lois and Tom managed to make a rather complete set of drawings, so we'll use them to illustrate our ideas.

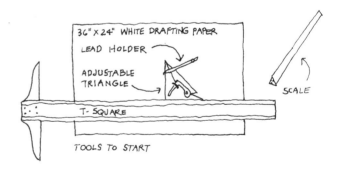

36" X 24" WHITE DRAFTING PAPER

LEAD HOLDER

ADJUSTABLE TRIANGLE

T-SQUARE

SCALE

TOOLS TO START

DRAWING YOUR FLOOR PLANS

Lois and Tom's floor plan, as they had developed on page 95, is a perfect illustration of the information you need to impart to interested parties, such as your building inspector, your contractor, your neighbors, your relatives, or even to yourself.

There are three easy rules in making these drawings:

1. Draw the plan using the symbols shown on page 92.
2. Show the important dimensions.
3. Letter your specification notes around the plan.

Now is the time to review your wish list, files, and scrapbook. Make sure you have labeled all of your best ideas and specified your favorite materials with notes on your drawings.

The opposite page shows Lois and Tom's floor plan, drawn with a T-square and triangle. They liked their free-hand sketch drawings but wanted these drawings to look more "professional." If you have a difficult time mastering these drafting tools, don't hesitate to use the "sketch" style that you developed during your design work.

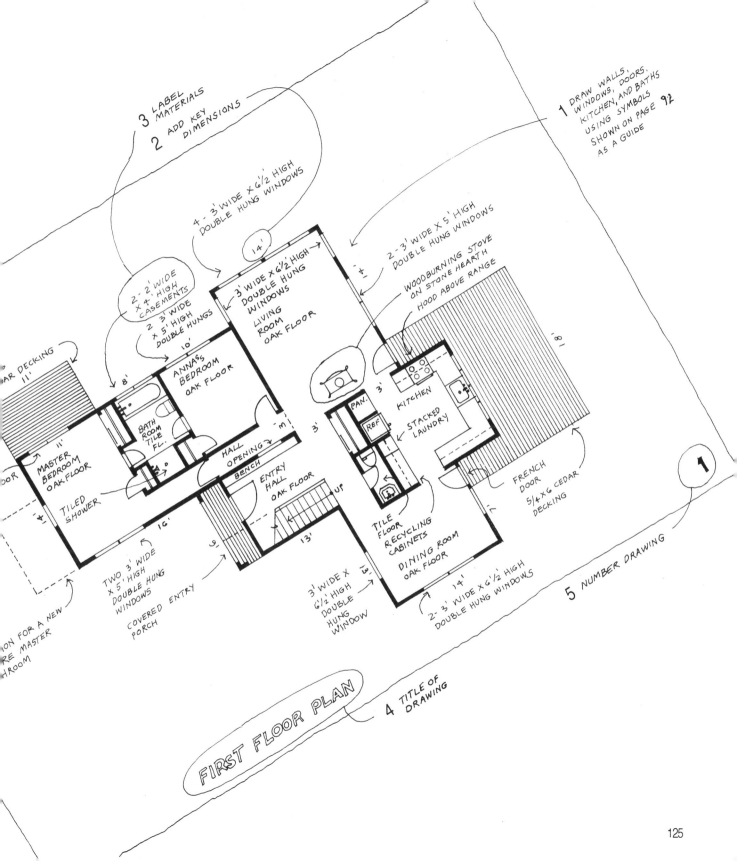

3 LABEL MATERIALS

2 ADD KEY DIMENSIONS

1 DRAW WALLS, WINDOWS, DOORS, KITCHEN, AND BATHS USING SYMBOLS SHOWN ON PAGE 92 AS A GUIDE

4 - 3' WIDE X 6½ HIGH DOUBLE HUNG WINDOWS

2 - 2' WIDE X 4' HIGH CASEMENTS

2 - 3' WIDE X 5' HIGH DOUBLE HUNGS

3' WIDE X 6½ HIGH DOUBLE HUNG WINDOWS

2 - 3' WIDE X 5' HIGH DOUBLE HUNG WINDOWS

WOODBURNING STOVE ON STONE HEARTH HOOD ABOVE RANGE

14'

LIVING ROOM OAK FLOOR

AR DECKING 11'

10'

ANNA'S BEDROOM OAK FLOOR

8'

BATH ROOM TILE FL.

11'

MASTER BEDROOM OAK FLOOR

TILED SHOWER

16'

HALL OPENING

BENCH

ENTRY HALL OAK FLOOR

3'

3'

KITCHEN

PAN.

REF.

STACKED LAUNDRY

TILE FLOOR RECYCLING CABINETS

DINING ROOM OAK FLOOR

8'

FRENCH DOOR 5/4 X 6 CEDAR DECKING

1

UP

13'

9'

ON FOR A NEW E MASTER HROOM

OR

TWO 3' WIDE X 5' HIGH DOUBLE HUNG WINDOWS

COVERED ENTRY PORCH

3' WIDE X 6½' HIGH DOUBLE HUNG WINDOW

13'

14'

2 - 3' WIDE X 6½ HIGH DOUBLE HUNG WINDOWS

5 NUMBER DRAWING

FIRST FLOOR PLAN

4 TITLE OF DRAWING

DRAWING YOUR ELEVATIONS

Elevations are the drawings of the exterior views of your design. The materials you plan to use on the outside of your house are usually specified in these drawings.

The next few pages will show the Samples' elevations and their exterior material choices. They have made these drawings on the 24" x 36" white drafting paper sheets at the same 1/4"=1'-0" scale used on their plans.

Once again, this is the time to consult your scrapbook and files to help you with your materials choices. Check your window sizes, and make sure you've specified the right cladding for the walls and roof. Don't hesitate to consult the Internet. You'll be living with these choices for a long time.

Your model will be a big help in visualizing your elevation drawings. Set it up on your site drawing so that you can see which side of your house faces north (north elevation), which side faces south (south elevation), and so on. Once you've completed the four elevations, you've drawn your entire house and, hopefully, noted all your favorite exterior materials.

Keep in mind that these drawings use a collection of graphic symbols, some of which are shown here.

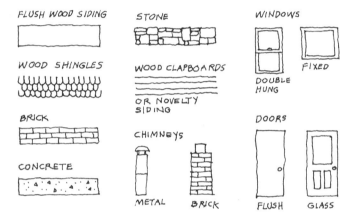

GRAPHIC SYMBOLS FOR ELEVATIONS

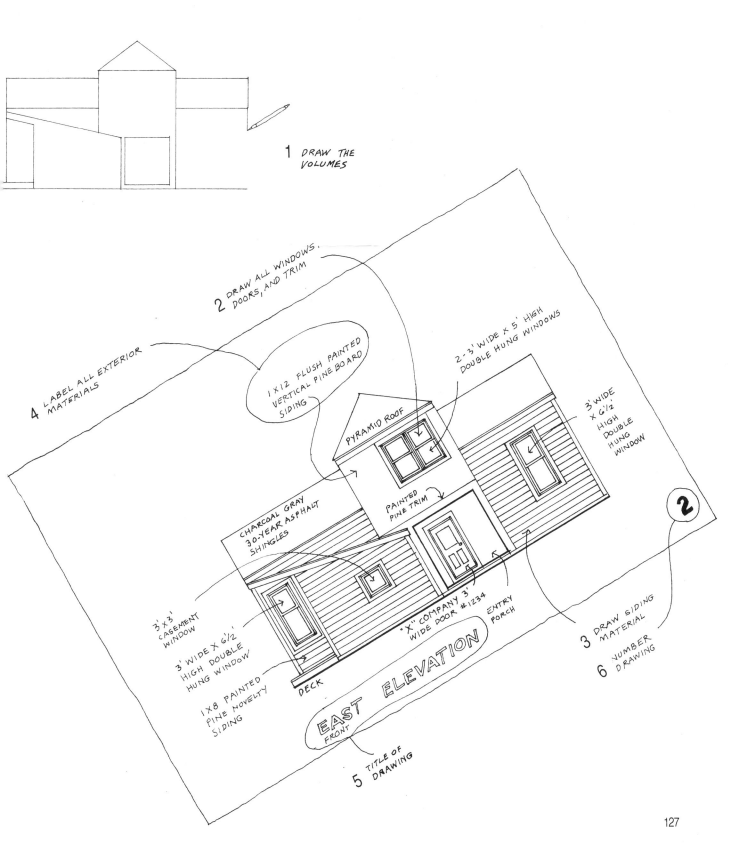

1 DRAW THE VOLUMES

2 DRAW ALL WINDOWS, DOORS, AND TRIM

4 LABEL ALL EXTERIOR MATERIALS

1X12 FLUSH PAINTED VERTICAL PINE BOARD SIDING

2-3' WIDE X 5' HIGH DOUBLE HUNG WINDOWS

3' WIDE X 6½' HIGH DOUBLE HUNG WINDOW

PYRAMID ROOF

CHARCOAL GRAY 30-YEAR ASPHALT SHINGLES

PAINTED PINE TRIM

3'X3' CASEMENT WINDOW

3' WIDE X 6½' HIGH DOUBLE HUNG WINDOW

1X8 PAINTED PINE NOVELTY SIDING

DECK

"X" COMPANY 3' WIDE DOOR #1234

ENTRY PORCH

3 DRAW SIDING MATERIAL

6 NUMBER DRAWING

EAST ELEVATION
FRONT

5 TITLE OF DRAWING

2

127

Here are two more of Lois and Tom's elevation drawings.
Notice how their model helps them to visualize their design.

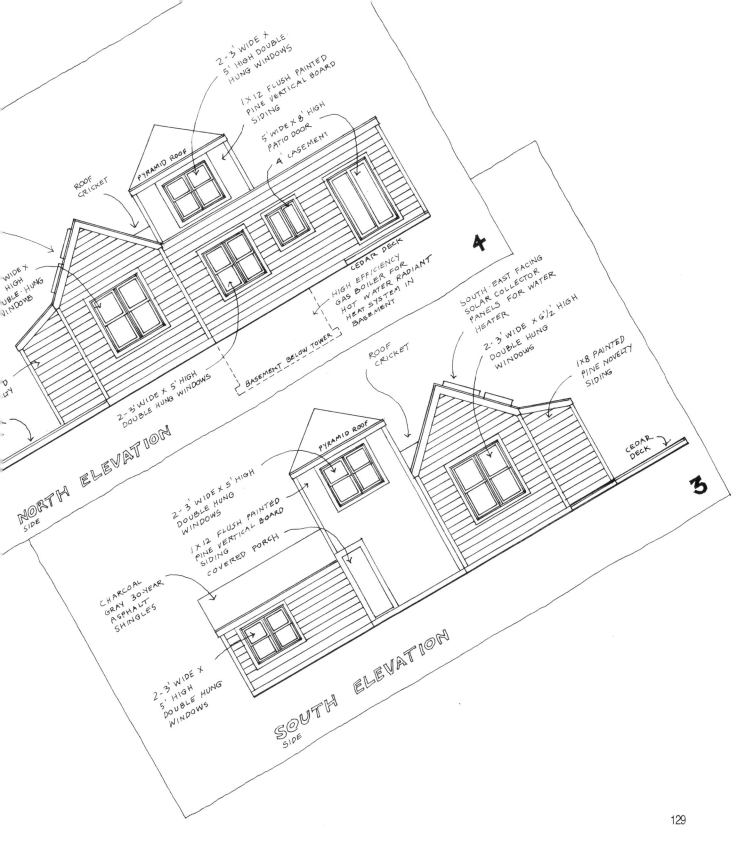

2-3' WIDE X 5' HIGH DOUBLE HUNG WINDOWS

1X12 FLUSH PAINTED PINE VERTICAL BOARD SIDING

5' WIDE X 8' HIGH PATIO DOOR

4' CASEMENT

PYRAMID ROOF

ROOF CRICKET

WIDE X HIGH UBLE HUNG WINDOWS

CEDAR DECK

HIGH EFFICIENCY GAS BOILER FOR HOT WATER RADIANT HEAT SYSTEM IN BASEMENT

BASEMENT BELOW TOWER

2-3' WIDE X 5' HIGH DOUBLE HUNG WINDOWS

NORTH ELEVATION
SIDE

SOUTH-EAST FACING SOLAR COLLECTOR PANELS FOR WATER HEATER

2-3' WIDE X 6½' HIGH DOUBLE HUNG WINDOWS

1X8 PAINTED PINE NOVELTY SIDING

CEDAR DECK

ROOF CRICKET

PYRAMID ROOF

2-3' WIDE X 5' HIGH DOUBLE HUNG WINDOWS

1X12 FLUSH PAINTED PINE VERTICAL BOARD SIDING

COVERED PORCH

CHARCOAL GRAY 30-YEAR ASPHALT SHINGLES

2-3' WIDE X 5' HIGH DOUBLE HUNG WINDOWS

SOUTH ELEVATION
SIDE

4

3

129

DRAWING YOUR SECTIONS

A section view is a cut-away or slice taken through a part of
your house. This drawing is useful in explaining the heights
of ceilings and the type of insulation in the floor, walls, and
ceiling. Again, sections use a collection of graphic symbols,
some of which are shown here.

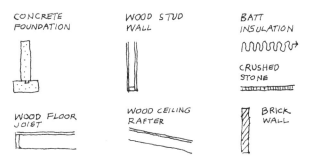

GRAPHIC SYMBOLS FOR SECTIONS

1 PICK YOUR MOST IMPORTANT
  SPACES TO DRAW AS
  SECTIONS

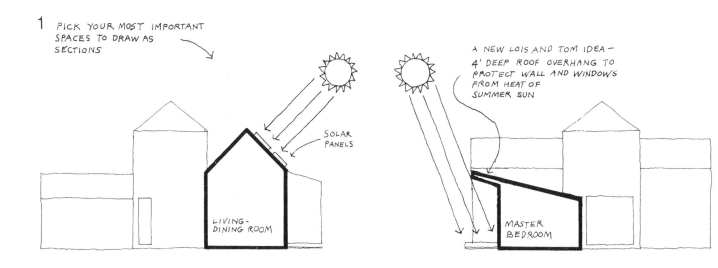

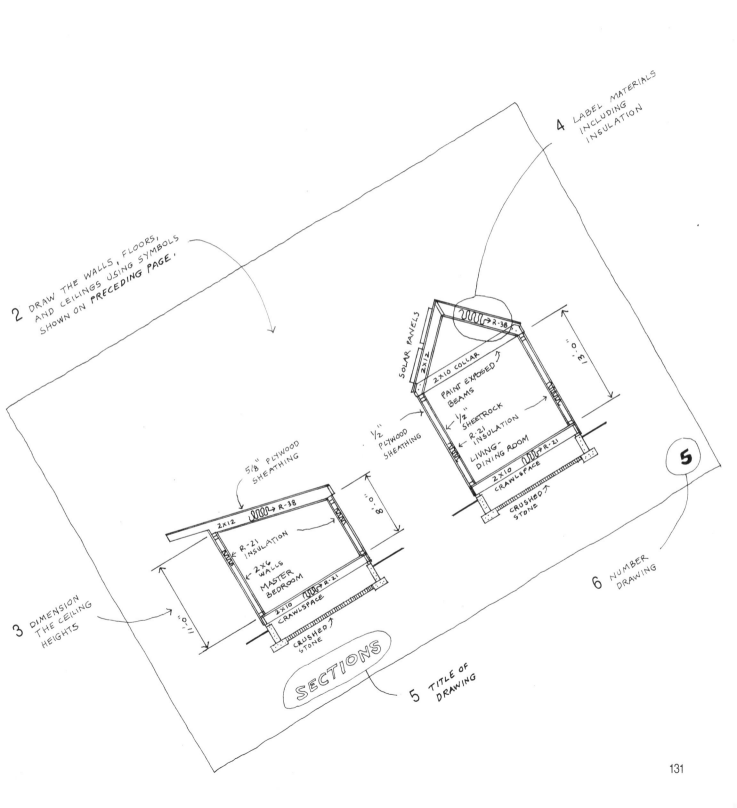

2 DRAW THE WALLS, FLOORS,
AND CEILINGS USING SYMBOLS
SHOWN ON **PRECEDING PAGE**,

4 LABEL MATERIALS
INCLUDING
INSULATION

5/8" PLYWOOD
SHEATHING

1/2" PLYWOOD
SHEATHING

SOLAR PANELS

2X12

2X10 COLLAR

PAINT EXPOSED
BEAMS

1/2" SHEETROCK

R-21 INSULATION

LIVING-
DINING ROOM

2X10 → R-21

CRAWLSPACE

R-38

13'-0"

CRUSHED STONE

5

2X12 → R-38

R-21
INSULATION

2X6 WALLS

MASTER
BEDROOM

R-21

CRAWLSPACE

8'-0"

2X10

CRUSHED STONE

11'-0"

3 DIMENSION
THE CEILING
HEIGHTS

6 NUMBER
DRAWING

SECTIONS

5 TITLE OF
DRAWING

131

FINISHING YOUR DRAWINGS

Once you've finished your plans, elevations, and sections, it's time to complete the set with a cover sheet. This is a good place to show the site plan that you developed in Chapter 3 because it provides a nice introduction to your project.

Take these drawings to a printer and get a few sets for some future meetings with builders and perhaps an architect or engineer. The builders will give you valuable information to add to the drawings and can help you with the requirements of your local building department. The architect or engineer will, for a fee, advise you as to whether your drawings are suitable to get a building permit, whether you need more information on the drawings, whether you need professional drawings using your drawings as a resource, or whether you even need a building permit. In any case, your drawings are your design and are the basis of you getting a new home that is personal, and designed by you.

Lois and Tom made four sets of prints of their completed drawings: two for their builder, one for an architect/engineer, and one for themselves. If they need to get a building permit, they'll get two more sets of prints later.

These sets of prints represent a great deal of time and energy, but now Tom and Lois can relax. They walk down to their empty building site and find that the feeling that a building of their design is soon to be erected is so rewarding and exciting. They know they will live happily ever after in their own "architect - designed" home.

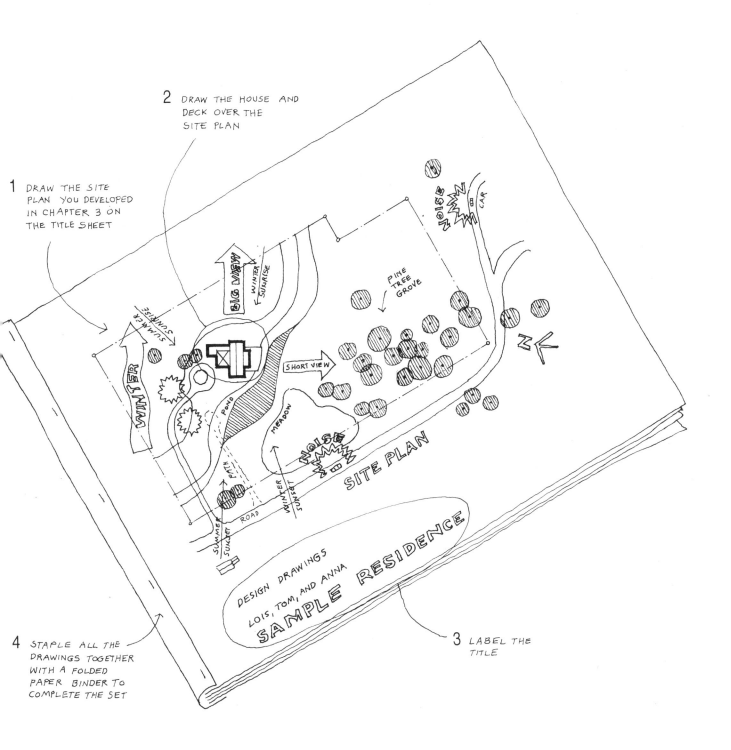

1 DRAW THE SITE
PLAN YOU DEVELOPED
IN CHAPTER 3 ON
THE TITLE SHEET

2 DRAW THE HOUSE AND
DECK OVER THE
SITE PLAN

3 LABEL THE
TITLE

4 STAPLE ALL THE
DRAWINGS TOGETHER
WITH A FOLDED
PAPER BINDER TO
COMPLETE THE SET

BIG VIEW

WINTER SUNRISE

SUMMER SUNRISE

WINTER

SHORT VIEW

PINE TREE GROVE

NOISE

CAR

NE

POND

MEADOW

NOISE

PATH

ROAD

WINTER SUNSET

SUMMER SUNSET

SITE PLAN

DESIGN DRAWINGS

LOIS, TOM, AND ANNA

SAMPLE RESIDENCE

Use your paper model to study how gabled volumes, which intersect each other here, can create a more sculptural design.

8 GETTING READY TO BUILD

This chapter briefly discusses how your drawings and model might help you in obtaining a building permit, if necessary; whether or not you need an architect or engineer to help you; and your relationship with your builder.

GETTING PERMISSION TO BUILD

In many communities, in order to build your home, you must first obtain permission from your local Building Department. This is done by filing a formal application with your drawings for your future house. If your design satisfies all local and state code requirements, a building permit is issued for a nominal fee.

1. If you live in a community that does not require a building permit, you should meet with a highly qualified and recommended builder to see if he can build your house using your drawings and model as a guide. If your drawings are less than what he needs for construction, he may want you to engage an architect or engineer to upgrade your work.

2. If you live in a community that requires a building permit, you should meet with the building inspector, tell him/her your story, and ask for recommendations for someone who can help you bring your drawings up to code. The inspector will probably recommend an architect or engineer who will make a new set of construction drawings (using your drawings as a guide), or simply red-line your drawings for you to change as he/she notes. In either case, the final set of drawings will have to meet the codes so that they can be stamped by the architect or engineer for approval by the building inspector.

Lois and Tom needed a permit and were advised to hire a local architect who would transform their drawings into a set of construction drawings suitable for building and for obtaining a permit. They were happy to find that their architect was able to conform to their design and found that most of the decisions they had made, in their drawings and with their model, were embraced in the final set of drawings.

They received their permit from the local building inspector and excitedly set off to meet with their builder.

BUILDING INSPECTOR

CONSTRUCTION AND SUPERVISION

No matter how much you and your contractor like each other (an important ingredient in this relationship), you should put in writing what each expects from the other. List any items not specifically shown on the drawings that you expect the contractor to do. Be sure to include a period of time during which you expect the house to be built. The amount, the timing, and the method of payment should be stated.

There are two common forms of this type of agreement. One is a fixed price for which the contractor agrees to provide everything shown on the drawings for one sum, stated before construction begins. The second method is where the contractor charges for his materials and an hourly amount to cover his labor and overhead. The fixed price agreement is usually more comfortable because you know, in advance, the final cost. The time and materials agreement can be less expensive if the project goes smoothly and you have a very honest builder.

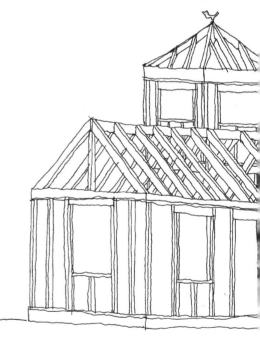

It is important to supervise construction to make sure that the work being billed for has actually been completed and to see that the drawings are being followed. Also, during construction you might be inspired to make a change that will make the project better or might save money.

Tom and Lois have hired a wonderful builder who is a family friend and is well known for his excellent craftsmanship throughout the region. They have made a written agreement that they are happy with and expect to have the time of their lives building their dream house.

A deck can be an inexpensive and important extension of your living spaces on the viewside of your home.

ACKNOWLEDGMENTS

Thank you to Jeff Milstein who co-authored the original 1976 edition of *Designing Houses* with me.

Thank you to the people at Overlook Press; Peter Mayer who has published all my books and has provided encouragement all along the way, and Stephanie Gorton for her continuous monitoring of the work.

A special acknowledgement goes to my wife Karen, who has acted as my guide and gentle critic with all phases of the book.

Finally, I owe a great deal to the hundreds of clients I've had the pleasure to work with during my many years as a practicing architect. They were and are the true inspiration for this book. They demonstrate to me how much it means to be involved in the process of creating one's home.

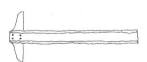

Careful design using colored volumes with an entry porch and thoughtful landscaping can configure an exciting home even on a very tight site.

OTHER BOOKS BY LESTER WALKER

American Shelter

Tiny Houses

The Tiny Book of Tiny Houses

Housebuilding for Children

Carpentry for Children

Block Building for Children